GOOD FOOD fast!

GOOD FOOD fast!

Deliciously Healthy Gluten-Free Meals for People on the Go

CHEF JASON ROBERTS

WITH STACEY COLINO   PHOTOGRAPHS BY SAMI JOHNSON

LYONS PRESS
Guilford, Connecticut
Helena, Montana
An imprint of Rowman & Littlefield

Lyons Press is an imprint of Rowman & Littlefield

Distributed by NATIONAL BOOK NETWORK

Text copyright © 2015 by Jason Roberts
Photographs copyright © 2015 by Sami Johnson

Jacques Apple recipe on page 229 courtesy of Jacques Pépin, Houghton Mifflin Harcourt. Eve's Chocolate Cake recipe on page 220 courtesy of Damien Pignolet.

British Library Cataloging-in-Publication Information available

Library of Congress Cataloging-in-Publication Data

Roberts, Jason (Chef)
  Good food—fast! : deliciously healthy gluten-free meals for people on the go / Jason Roberts with Stacey Colino ; photographs by Sami Johnson.
     pages cm
  Summary: "If you want to eat healthy without sacrificing flavor but are so busy that you often find yourself resorting to takeout or packaged convenience foods, this book is for you! Chef Jason Roberts shows how eating a rainbow of fruits and vegetables and other nutritious foods can fuel our bodies and minds—and still excite our palates." — Provided by publisher.
  Includes bibliographical references and index.
  ISBN 978-1-4930-0823-0 (hardback)
1. Quick and easy cooking. I. Colino, Stacey. II. Title.
  TX833.5.R585 2014
  641.5'12—dc23
                                                                                          2014031668

∞™ The paper used in this publication meets the minimum requirements of American National Standard for Information Sciences—Permanence of Paper for Printed Library Materials, ANSI/NISO Z39.48-1992.

FOR THE BOYS . . .
MY SON HUNTER
AND MY NEPHEWS LEVI,
SAM, AND BRANSON

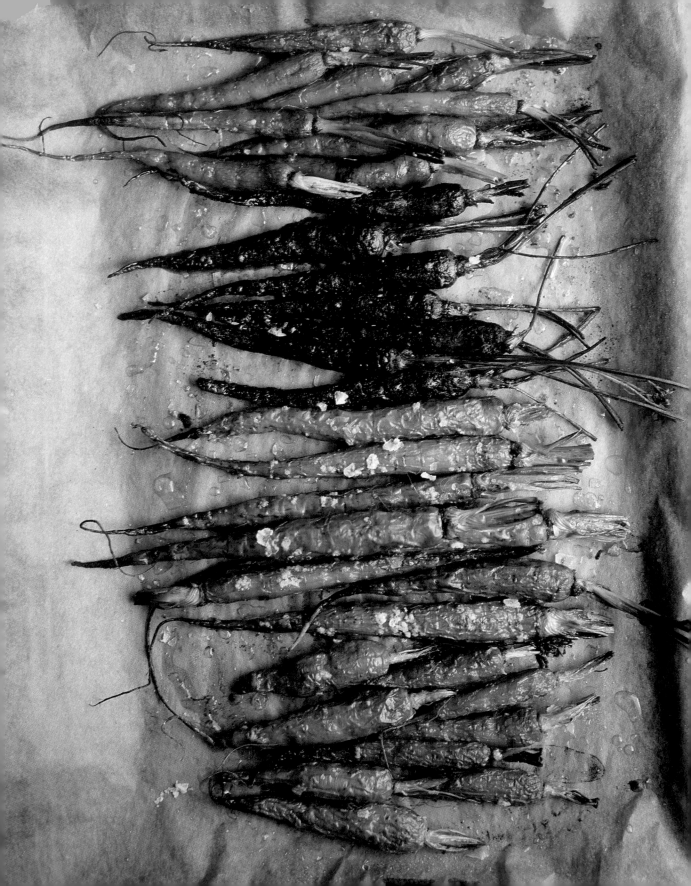

CONTENTS

INTRODUCTION

It often seems like an overwhelming challenge to cook a homemade meal when we're already juggling a full plate of responsibilities. With a perpetually rushed lifestyle, it's an unfortunate conundrum we've all encountered! When it comes to cooking at home, many of us have a love it-or-leave-it mind-set: It's quick, easy, affordable, and already packaged, or it's a trip to five different stores to buy costly ingredients only to then slave away for hours in the kitchen trying to create the meal. (Personally, that would drive me nuts!) We believe food is either healthy or delicious but unlikely to be both. Many of us will stay within our cooking comfort zones or feel the need to enroll in a culinary school to upgrade our techniques before we're willing to even attempt to cut up a whole chicken.

Breathe! It's going to be okay—I promise. The truth is, I can totally sympathize, but to my way of thinking, these are all unnecessary burdens. You really *can* prepare delicious, nutritious meals in the comfort of your own home with a minimal time commitment, a reasonable budget, and just one trip to the grocery store or farmers' market. The key is to be prepared, organized, and efficient in your shopping and cooking techniques.

> The food going into your body provides the energy your body expends, so you'll want to make it top-quality fuel.

Healthy living and eating have always been passions of mine. I grew up in a family of food professionals and learned to cook and appreciate the value of food at a young age in both Australia and New Zealand. I've been doing it ever since—in restaurants, on the telly, on the radio, through print media, social media, live food shows around the world, and, of course, in my own kitchen. I live it, I breathe it, and I certainly cook it! As a chef who travels often, I have discovered that my health and my ability to maintain focus depend entirely on what I eat and how I exercise. For as long as I can remember, I have been super active—as a cyclist, surfer, swimmer, and runner, not to mention dad—so I tend to look at food as fuel, as well as a source of pleasure.

The food going into your body provides the energy your body expends, so you'll want to make it top-quality fuel. As I've gotten older, I've come to realize just how much of a gross misjudgment it is to leave the day's food selections to chance. The right foods will give you the right energy to power through the day. The wrong foods . . . *well, who even wants to think about that?!* The point is, if you plan better, you can eat better. It's as simple as that.

As a cook/chef/lover of food, I have a deep, abiding appreciation for the importance of incorporating varied tastes and textures and using simple cooking methods and techniques when preparing meals. Over the years, I have discovered that with the proper planning and preparation, it is possible to put together healthy, delicious meals that are loaded with tantalizing flavors, textures, and aromas in very little time. It's a matter of being conscious of fresh, vibrant ingredients, using a variety of colors from Mother Nature's garden, and relying on low-moisture cooking techniques (such as roasting, sautéing, steaming, and stir-frying, all of which will preserve what Mother Nature intended as far as the goodness, nutrients, flavors, colors, and textures of your fresh ingredients) to get the job done—with a minimum of fuss. This book will show you how to do this in your own kitchen.

The trick is to choose foods that will fuel and strengthen your body and mind, while letting their flavors and textures delight your taste buds and inspire you. In general, I have figured out that simpler is usually better: Not only will the food look better but it also will taste better and be better for you. Be sure to use good-quality ingredients and be conscious of your cooking methods. I have learned how to incorporate all of these elements in the meals I prepare for myself, my friends, and loved ones, and it is my personal quest to teach you how to cook this way as well.

The old adage that you should never trust a skinny chef—since chefs generally use plenty of fat, salt, and sugar to make their meals memorable—no longer rings true. Once I reached the age of thirty-five, I found that I really needed to tune into what I was eating—both the types of food and the portion sizes. By eating well and exercising more (and avoiding gluten since I'm gluten intolerant), I improved my body composition by dropping body fat and increasing muscle mass.

With the increasing rates of lifestyle-related chronic diseases, many chefs, cooks, and consumers alike are beginning to realize it's time to start taking their health seriously and become more conscious of what's in their food. While many of us get to pick and choose what we eat and how and when we do so, on the whole a large proportion of us don't seem to be doing it right. Consider this: In the United States, 69 percent of adults, ages twenty and older, are considered overweight or obese, according to the Centers for Disease Control and Prevention. Heart disease is the leading killer of men and women in the United States, and obesity and poor eating habits increase the risk of heart disease and stroke significantly. Obesity is also a major risk factor for type 2 diabetes and many forms of cancer.

So it really is wise to consume healthy meals for the sake of weight management and your health. To me, cooking has and always will be the most consistent of life's joys: I do it to indulge my passion and share it with friends and family, but the more I think about it, and the older and wiser that I get, the more conscious I am that cooking

provides the food that will keep me nourished. Every meal that I eat, now that I have crossed over the forty-year mark (I know: I still look twenty-one—wink, wink), really affects the way I feel, look, sleep, and dream. It affects my energy, my concentration, and my metabolism, so eating well is key!

In my opinion, a good home-cooked meal will always outweigh anything you could buy already prepared. Not only does home cooking allow you to control every ingredient that goes into your meal, but there is absolutely no need for colorings, preservatives, or chemical emulsifiers when you cook for you and your family. With the right simple, healthy ingredients and a dash of daring and confidence, cooking at home allows you to create flavorful dishes that will impress your palate and nourish your body, mind, and spirit. Learning to cook in a way that will tempt your taste buds, while sticking within a budget and a reasonable timetable, will enable you to embark on your own personal food revolution. Once you do, you'll never look back, just like I haven't. The recipes in this book were created with these goals in mind—and they

will help you raise the bar on everyday food preparation to a whole new level.

Good Food—Fast! will show you how to think outside of the box or package when it comes to preparing breakfast, lunch, and dinner, and how to use both healthy and fun cooking techniques that will preserve the inherent nutrients that are present in foods that come directly from Mother Nature. Once you master the techniques and recipes, cooking healthy and delicious meals will become a breeze—and a true joy for you, your family, and your friends.

I firmly believe that working together in the kitchen and sharing mealtimes fosters deeper connections between people. Preparing and sharing delicious food with those you care about creates a sense of comfort and pleasure and brings people together in enchanting ways. Plus, if you use healthy ingredients and thoughtful cooking techniques, you'll be making a smart investment in your health and well-being for the long run. It's a no-lose proposition, really. So roll up those sleeves and get in the kitchen. It's time to eat your way to a healthier lifestyle!

> Choose foods that will fuel and strengthen your body and mind, while their flavors and textures will delight your taste buds.

CHAPTER ONE
FUELING UP

While I have always been physically active, it's only as I've grown older that I've really begun to appreciate the importance of using food as a source of fuel. If you put poor-quality food into your body, you won't achieve the performance you're striving for each day. On the flip side, if you treat your body to high-octane fuel—in the form of highly nutritious foods—you'll increase your chances of having plenty of energy, strength, concentration, stamina, and other measures of optimal performance. By upgrading my eating habits, I have found that I sleep better, I have more energy and feel terrific throughout the day, my concentration is better, and when I look in the mirror, it reflects the positive physical changes.

Food supplies the building blocks for every organ and function in the body from head to toe: Protein is necessary for proper muscle development and maintenance, carbohydrates provide quick and sustainable forms of energy, healthy fats are required for hormonal production and healthy skin and hair, and so on. The nutritious foods you ingest now will also limit the amount of medications you will need later.

The foods Mother Nature offers are perfectly packaged, which is why I use a lot of fruits, vegetables, nuts, and seeds in my cooking. Maybe this is partly because ingredients that come from Mother Nature's garden bear a surprising resemblance to organs in the body. Think about it: Walnuts resemble the human brain, a tomato has four chambers just like the heart, sweet potatoes look a lot like the pancreas, long stalks of celery and bok choy mirror bones, a sliced carrot resembles an eye, and gingerroot looks a bit like a stomach. Interestingly enough, each of these foods contributes in important ways to the healthy function and integrity of the organs they resemble. For example, the omega-3 fatty acids in walnuts help support cognitive function and mood stability. The lycopene in tomatoes is good for your heart. The beta-carotene in sweet potatoes protects the pancreas (and other organs) from cellular damage. Carrots contain antioxidant vitamins (like beta-carotene) that help decrease the risk of developing macular degeneration (a leading cause of vision loss as people get older). And ginger can actually soothe an irritated stomach, quelling indigestion or nausea.

Moreover, raw or cooked vegetables and fruits are rich sources of nutrients, antioxidants, and other phytochemicals (plant-based compounds that promote good health and can reduce the risk of cancer and other chronic diseases). I incorporate foods that tend to be lower on the glycemic index (meaning, they produce a lower and slower rise in blood sugar levels than foods that rank higher on the glycemic index) and foods that have anti-inflammatory properties, since chronic inflammation can increase the risk of heart disease, type 2 diabetes, stroke, Alzheimer's disease, and some forms of cancer. Food really is medicine. After my dad was diagnosed with type 2 diabetes, he improved his diet and managed to reverse his diabetes in three months. That's right—just by eating more healthfully and getting more exercise, he was able to get rid of diabetes *without having to take medication.*

As you know by now, I'm a big believer in exercise, not just to prevent or reverse health conditions but because staying physically active enhances weight management and overall wellness. When it comes right down to it, living well is about making good food and exercise choices all the time (apart from the occasional lapse). If you feel like you don't have time to exercise, there are some basic things you can do in just fifteen minutes a day to improve your fitness level; you'll find my strategies along these lines in the appendix.

For the sake of our health and well-being, it's important to choose ingredients and meals wisely. While food is fuel for the body and mind, it's also so much more than that: a way to express love and nurture others, a source of pleasure and creativity, and a feast for the senses, among other things. And yet many of us are in such a perpetual rush that we don't give meal preparation the attention it deserves. Eating well need not be boring, tasteless, or time-consuming. In fact, it can be the exact opposite—but only when we move away from the stereotypical format of breakfast, lunch, and dinner. With a little imagination, creativity, and advance planning, your life can truly open up to the world of gloriously rewarding foods.

Many people have a tendency to stick with a few tried-and-true dishes, and because of time constraints and a limited skill base, they will rarely venture outside their comfort zone in the kitchen. For example, I have heard many people say they won't cook fish for fear of spoiling an expensive piece of seafood, or that they won't buy exotic vegetables they're not familiar with because they don't know what to do with them. As Michael Pollan, the author of *In Defense of Food: An Eater's Manifesto*, noted in a recent lecture I watched on the Internet, "We have been brainwashed to think of cooking as drudgery." I also believe many people think cooking is best left to the professionals; in other words, they don't trust themselves to do it right, which may partly explain why the practice of home cooking in the United States has dropped by 50 percent since the mid-1960s.

It's easy enough to get over this fear factor if you learn the right tips and tricks on how to prep, season, test, taste, and use good sense (with a dash of logic) in

The Healing Power of Herbs and Spices

Besides adding flavor and dimension to your meals, various herbs and spices offer considerable health benefits. Cinnamon has antioxidant and anti-inflammatory properties, and it has been found to help regulate blood sugar. Cloves are also loaded with antioxidant and anti-inflammatory effects, as well as antimicrobial compounds. Coriander is a strong digestive aid and has antibacterial properties that can help fight food-borne bacteria. Fennel is also a potent digestion enhancer, and it can reduce bad breath. Ginger has strong anti-inflammatory effects, as well as an ability to reduce indigestion and nausea and help with pain relief (from migraines, for example). Oregano has impressive antibacterial properties, and rosemary is packed with compounds that have antibacterial effects that can help fight infection. Sage has been found to enhance memory function and protect the brain from changes that can lead to certain forms of dementia; it also has anti-inflammatory and antioxidant effects. Turmeric is a powerful digestive aid and it has strong anti-inflammatory effects to boot, making it a potentially potent weapon against cancer. So go ahead and start thinking of these herbs and spices as the cures in your kitchen!

the kitchen. Keep in mind that the premise behind *Good Food—Fast!* isn't to create the home-based version of fast food. When it comes to food preparation, *fast* is a relative term. While there may be a bit of a time investment in, say, braising a chicken, roasting vegetables or meats, poaching fruits, or baking other ingredients, if you make enough of these items at any given time, you can divvy up the amount and use them in multiple dishes, hence saving time in the long run. An added bonus: You'll be practicing portion control, which is an essential element in eating healthfully and managing your weight. In the pages that follow, I'll show you how to do all this. *I promise!*

Plan Better, Cook Better, Eat Better

When it comes to making good food fast, it's essential to plan ahead. It's important to shop wisely for your ingredients and to keep certain staples on hand. Having taken the gluten-free road a few years ago, my pantry has evolved over time. These days, you will not find any form of gluten in my cupboards. But you may find items you've never heard of (such as raw cacao, maca root powder, and asafetida). Having said that, I believe there are certain ingredients that should stock every pantry. These include almond milk, cans of beans (chickpeas, black beans, and others), chia seeds, flaxseeds, dried organic beans and legumes (like lentils), quinoa, canned tomatoes, canned sardines and tuna, various types of rice (brown, wild, basmati, Arborio), various vinegars (red wine, sherry, balsamic, white) and oils (canola, sunflower, walnut, and extra-virgin olive oil), different nuts (including almonds, walnuts, and hazelnuts), dried fruits (figs, dates, apricots), steel-cut oats, tapioca starch, cornstarch, polenta, rice flour, sriracha hot sauce, tamari (gluten-free soy) sauce, vanilla extract, and a selection of herbs and spices, including black and white pepper, cinnamon, cloves, coriander seed, cumin, dried chili flakes, fennel seeds, mustard seeds, nutmeg, oregano, and rosemary.

At a minimum, a cook's refrigerator should always contain butter, eggs, mayonnaise, mustard (both the whole-grain and smooth varieties), yogurt, and various fruits and vegetables. When it comes to produce, seasonality plays such a big role in its pricing—and also the flavor. It has become terribly confusing, seeing as we can now import pretty much anything we like since there is a demand for it. But that doesn't mean fruits and vegetables will be at their most nutritious or flavorful best all year long. The following is a guide to the produce that is freshest during the four seasons:

- Strawberries, for example, are always best in the summer, even though they are accessible pretty much every day of the year. The same is true of avocados, blackberries, blueberries, raspberries, cherries, corn, cucumbers, melons, peaches and nectarines, tomatoes, summer squash, and zucchini.

- Fall is the time when cranberries, eggplant, grapes, mushrooms, okra, parsnips, peppers, persimmons, and pomegranates are at their best.

- In the winter months, beets, cabbage, clementines, fennel, grapefruit, and winter squash are more widely available (and at better prices).

- Spring is prime time for asparagus, fava beans, fiddleheads, mint, morels, peas, radishes, ramps, rhubarb, and sweet onions.

Meanwhile, some fruits and vegetables—such as apples, broccoli, carrots, cauliflower, many lettuces, and pears—are widely available year-round. Knowing what's in season can help you choose as many fruits and vegetables as possible that are at the peak of their nutritional vitality and their natural flavorful best.

The challenge after selecting the best ingredients you can find is to develop a sound understanding of cooking techniques. Once you do, you can pretty much master any and every recipe you'd ever want to try. Before you can get cooking, though, you need to make sure you have the right tools available. Your kitchen doesn't need to be outfitted like a professional kitchen, but some basic equipment is in order, including flat-bottomed nonstick skillets or sauté pans (10 inches and 12 inches in diameter) with lids, various sizes of saucepans and pots, baking dishes, cake pans, a cake rack, cookie trays, roasting pans, a wok, and a griddle plate (for indoor grilling). You'll also want to have cutting boards, a selection of mixing bowls, a set of measuring cups and measuring spoons, as well as an electric mixer, a blender, a food processor, and perhaps a juicer. In addition, you should have a good chef's knife, a few paring knives, a sharpening tool to keep your knives sharp (this is a safety issue, too!), a Microplane (for grating cheese, citrus zest, and more), a cheese grater, a vegetable peeler, a mandoline slicer, a fine-mesh sieve and strainer, a metal skewer (for testing doneness), wooden skewers, a spatula, a wooden spoon, a slotted spoon, and a ladle. Be sure to have parchment (baking) paper and aluminum foil available for certain cooking methods, too.

The Inside Scoop on Techniques

Good cooking techniques can make all the difference in the outcome of a particular dish or meal. Rule number one: Be sure a skillet, sauté pan, or the oven is hot enough before you add ingredients; otherwise, the dish won't cook at the rate that it should, nor will it develop the color or texture you want it to. It's also essential to monitor the level of heat (the intensity of the flame on a gas stove or the inherent heat on an electric burner) while you're cooking, and to make sure a dish is the right distance from a heat source (while broiling, for example).

Cooking temperatures in modern-day ovens can vary considerably from one manufacturer and model to another. It's important to realize this because it doesn't take much to dry out a chicken while it's roasting or to undercook a cake if you're not prepared to look, feel, and engage your senses with what you are cooking. In the recipes that follow, you will see that I have been quite specific with times and temperatures, since most modern ovens can be set according to 5°F increments. The temperatures and times provided are definitely a good guide, but it's important for you to get to know your own oven and adjust the cooking times or temperatures accordingly.

Different cooking methods use different oven temperatures. Here's a quick look at how they stack up:

- Baking: 350°–375°F (175°–190°C)

- Resting/warming: 215°F (100°C)

- Roasting: 400°F (205°C)

- Slow cooking: 285°F (140°C)

Most people know how to boil, bake, or steam foods. Here's what you need to know about the basics of other cooking techniques:

Blanching: With this technique, foods—usually vegetables or fruits—are plunged into boiling water, removed after a prescribed interlude (usually 1 to 5 minutes, depending on the fruit or vegetable), then submerged into ice water or placed under cold running water to halt the cooking process (this is sometimes referred to as "refreshing" the food). This allows the asparagus, broccoli, brussels sprouts, cauliflower, green or yellow beans, or other food to maintain its natural color and freshness without getting soggy; plus, it prepares the item quickly or precooks it if it's being added to another dish.

Braising: It starts out like sautéing—since you brown the food in a bit of butter or oil—but then you add liquid (such as water or broth) to the pan or pot, cover it, and continue cooking it over low heat, either on the stove top or in the oven. Both methods are effective, as long as the ingredients you are cooking are submerged in liquid. (My mum used a slow cooker, which is great because it lets you cook at a constant temperature over a long period of time.) The time it takes to braise will vary depending on the ingredient: Vegetables will obviously take a lot less cooking time than a large cut of meat or dried beans.

Broiling: One of the keys to broiling successfully is to place the food at the right distance from the heat source. With thinner cuts of meat, poultry, or fish (less than an inch thick), you'll be able to get a crisp, brown exterior while roasting close (2 to 6 inches) to the flame. Thicker cuts, on the other hand, are likely to burn on the outside before they are cooked all the way through; that's why it's smart to move the thicker food to a lower rack, farther from the flame, so it browns a bit more slowly while having the chance to cook fully inside.

Grilling: It's a great form of low-moisture cooking that uses direct heat, allowing you to preserve the food's inherent nutritional goodness and add a caramelized flavor in the cooking process. Many people in the United States think of grilling for meats, but you can also grill vegetables and seafood. Starting the grilling process with a high temperature is important so that the food will cook quickly. Be careful not to overcook your food to the point of overcharring it or drying it out. Keep a watchful eye as you grill!

Poaching: A gentler technique than boiling, poaching involves submerging an item in a liquid (such as stock, broth, or water) that is barely simmering, rather than showing signs of visible bubbling (which would indicate a rolling boil). During the summer months, I poach copious amounts of stone fruits such as peaches and nectarines. In the winter, I poach pears, quinces, and rhubarb. Poached fruits lend themselves well to breakfast, desserts, smoothies, and delicious little snacks. I have never been a big fan of poaching fish and meat, purely because I love the flavors that are derived from roasting these items. When it comes to poaching everything except eggs—I like to drop eggs into simmering water so they cook quickly—it's always better to start by putting the item into a pot with cold water, bring it to a boil, then drop the temperature to a mere simmer. Cooking times will always vary, depending on the ripeness of the fruit or vegetable, or how aged, tough, or large the piece of meat or fish you are cooking. I find this is where a metal skewer comes in handy: Testing for resistance is a better indication than following a recipe guideline that doesn't take into account the quality of the ingredient, its texture, season, and other critical factors. When a food is cooked just right, you'll feel much less resistance on the skewer than when it's raw.

Roasting: Given our constant time constraints and the fact that we're on the go most of the time, roasting is an excellent cooking method that lends itself to pretty much anything—from roasted fruits or vegetables to meats or fish. As far as flavor goes, I love the caramelized smokiness that's achieved when ingredients are roasted at a high temperature. Having said that, when roasting meat on a high heat, you need to allow plenty of resting time so that the meat continues to cook without drying out the juices. Friends often ask me, "How come your chicken always tastes so moist?" The answer is, I don't keep it in the oven for 4 hours. I will roast a 3-pound chicken (with the backbone removed and an incision between the drumstick and thigh) flat, skin side down, at 400°F/205°C for 30 to 35 minutes in my oven and then let it rest for another 10 to 15 minutes. This helps it stay moist and tender.

Sautéing and stir-frying: With either of these methods—which are pretty much the same thing, to my way of thinking—you are cooking over direct heat, often using a small amount of fat, whether it's in a pan, a sauté pan, a frying pan, or a wok. In my kitchen, these pans are all used for cooking meals quickly; however, the wok is my go-to pan because it's so versatile. I even use my wok (over a medium-high heat) to dry-roast spices or fry aromatics in a little vegetable oil. For me, the general rule of thumb when sautéing or stir-frying is to add a little vegetable oil (such as olive oil, rice bran oil, coconut oil, or canola oil), your fragrant ingredients (such as onions, garlic, or ginger), then the protein (whether it's seafood, beef, lamb, pork, or poultry), and lightly cook these ingredients; then, I remove them from the pan and add my hardest vegetables (such as carrots, celery, or sweet potato), followed by the softer ones (such as spinach, asparagus, or broccoli), and a little bit of moisture (in the form of water or chicken stock, for example). Once these start cooking, I'll return the protein and any additional seasonings to heat all the ingredients together. Then it's serving time! A wok-cooked meal will literally take a matter of minutes, provided you have done a little preparation in advance.

Food Storage Basics

I don't know about you, but when I was a kid I would frequently open the refrigerator door and just stare at the food inside, contemplating whether or not I was hungry (I pretty much always was!). There were times I would get a stern rebuke: "Get out of the fridge, Jason!" Little did I know at the time that opening and closing the fridge allowed warm air in, causing the temperature inside to fluctuate, thereby allowing the food's temperature to fluctuate. It wasn't until later in life, when I began my culinary career, that I really grew to understand the importance of storing food correctly! Cross-contamination of foods and many food-borne illnesses could quite easily be dodged with just a little common sense and understanding how to pack, prepare, store, and rotate your food properly in the fridge. (To prepare for this task, be sure to have plenty of ziplock bags, storage containers, plastic wrap, and aluminum foil on hand.) All things considered, here are the best ways to store different foodstuffs in your fridge.

Meat, Fish, and Poultry: Keep these items in their store-packed wrapping, if possible. Unless the packaging is damaged or you want to break the package down into small quantities for freezing, there's no reason to unwrap and rewrap, which will simply increase the chances the food will be exposed to potentially harmful bacteria. For larger pieces of meat or poultry, I like to place them on a tray or plate to avoid any potential leakages in the fridge; I store these items on the lowest shelf above the crisper drawers (since this tends to be the coldest part of the fridge; warm air rises). Meat, seafood, and poultry are generally the most expensive commodities in your fridge, so preservation is essential, not just for the sake of eliminating bacteria, but also to reduce waste and loss of money.

Dairy Products: There's no good reason to remove any dairy items from their original packaging, unless you want to freeze some sticks of butter or put some portions into a smaller container to save space in your fridge; in that case, I recommend you also label and date the product with the use-by date on the package. I store my milk on the lowest possible shelf in the fridge and cheese and yogurt around the same level, again since this is the coolest part of the fridge. If you have a cheese and butter compartment in your fridge, it's fine to place these items there. Dairy products are susceptible to quick bacteria growth, so be careful with storage, and try not to leave that fridge door open too long!

Fruit and Vegetables: I use the crispers in my fridge to store fruit and vegetables. I keep them separate, as I find fruit will deteriorate a lot quicker than the vegetables do (except for green leafy vegetables). It's a big no-no to wash your lettuces, herbs, and greens before storing them, because exposure to the additional water can cause them to break down even more quickly. Since I generally shop for produce every three or four days, I don't need to overload my fridge with them! If your vegetable crispers are full, then I suggest using the top shelf for additional storage; that way, you can keep meats, fish, poultry, and dairy products on the lower, cooler shelves.

One common mistake many people make is putting hot food into the fridge, shortly after it's been cooked. Your refrigerator should be sitting steadily at a temperature of 40°F or below and the freezer at 0°F or below. Placing hot food in an overcrowded fridge is a disaster waiting to happen. At room temperature, bacteria have the ability to multiply in food every 20 minutes. So if you have a small fridge and you put something hot into it, you are likely to increase the temperature to a hazardous zone, which is anywhere between 42.8°F and 140°F—the perfect temperature for bacteria to grow and thrive! (Just to be on the safe side, I always have an additional thermometer sitting on the top shelf of my fridge so I know the fridge is maintaining a temperature of 40°F or below.) I suggest you allow your food to cool down before packing it away. Things like sauces, soups, and broths can be cooled by placing the pot into a large bowl of ice water to speed up the chilling process; something that has been baked (like lasagnas, casseroles, and meats) needs to cool to room temperature before it can be wrapped well and refrigerated.

As heartening as it is to see a fully stocked fridge, try to avoid overfilling it: In order for food to remain properly chilled, cool air needs to circulate throughout the fridge, and it can't do that if the fridge is packed to the gills.

Preserving the Longevity of Leftovers

Have you ever heard the saying that the most expensive ingredient in your fridge is the one you're about to throw out? I've spent years living by that maxim. I hate throwing out food, especially when I've spent time and energy shopping for ingredients or cooking a delicious meal. That's why I always make a good-faith effort to use up leftovers. The truth is most leftovers easily lend themselves to stir-fries, salads, omelets, and more, so there's no good reason to toss them.

But it is important to handle them properly. As far as storage goes, it's imperative that you place all leftovers in airtight containers or wrap them well. The best approach is to divide your leftovers into small, flat containers so they can cool off more quickly. Be sure the food has cooled before you seal and refrigerate the containers; otherwise, you're basically creating a petri dish for bacterial growth. If you're storing leftover roasted chicken or turkey, remove the stuffing and store it in a separate container. This will help the cooked bird cool properly and prevent bacteria buildup in the cavity where the stuffing was cooked. Keep in mind that rice can carry a particular form of bacteria (called *Bacillus cereus*) that can make you sick to your stomach. Some of the bacteria can survive the cooking process and multiply rapidly if rice is left at room temperature, so if you're not going to eat the rice right after cooking it, refrigerate it as quickly as possible (definitely within 3 hours). When you're ready to eat it, reheat it thoroughly. Never eat rice cold from the fridge, and don't keep any rice longer than two days.

> Food supplies the building blocks for every organ and function in the body from head to toe

In general, it's important to refrigerate leftovers within 2 hours of cooking or removing it from an appliance (such as a hot plate) that's been used to keep it warm. To prevent bacterial growth, cool the food rapidly so it reaches a safe-storage temperature in the fridge (40°F or below). To do this, divide large amounts of food (such as a big pot of soup or a casserole) into smaller, shallow containers or place the pot in an ice- or cold-water bath, or divide large cuts of meat into smaller parts, then refrigerate. Typically, leftovers can be kept safely in the refrigerator for three to four days or frozen for three to four months. When you reheat them—whether it's on the stove, in the oven, or in the microwave—make sure the food gets heated all the way through (to 165°F/75°C) to kill any lingering bacteria.

These may seem like mundane issues to be concerned about, but if you're spending money and time on good foods and expending energy preparing them at home, it makes sense to protect your investment. Besides, getting a food-borne illness is no fun at all! So protect your health, along with your investment, by being cautious and conscientious about the way you store and handle your food for your and your family's sake.

The recipes that follow will help you get in the habit of cooking foods that are good for you and that taste good, too. By eating this way, you'll be fueling your body with essential nutrients, boosting your energy, strength, and concentration in the process. You'll be able to eat healthfully without sacrificing flavor or busting your budget. And you'll learn to think outside of the box or package when it comes to preparing health-promoting meals and snacks. Once you master the techniques and recipes described in this book, cooking healthy and delicious meals will become a breeze— and a true joy for you, your family, and your friends. You can't go wrong here!

CHAPTER TWO
BREAK THE FAST!

Your mom was right: Breakfast really is the most important meal of the day. Overnight your body has fasted for a good chunk of time, provided you weren't sleepwalking and rummaging through the fridge in the wee hours of the night. Come morning, it's time to wake up your body and kick-start your metabolism, along with your energy and concentration levels. In fact, research suggests that the right breakfast foods can boost your performance in the classroom or at work, give you more strength and endurance for physical activities, and improve your ability to control your weight. So it's a mistake to skip breakfast; you'd be better off having a light meal if you tend not to be hungry in the morning than shirking it entirely. Otherwise, you might run out of fuel early in the day, lose focus, or become extremely peckish and overeat later.

Breakfast doesn't have to be a time-consuming proposition, but we need to get away from the idea that breakfast should come from a box. Many people stick with starchy breakfasts, which can give you quick energy but cause you to run out of steam quickly, too. It's important to include some protein in your morning meal for lasting fullness, vitality, and stamina. Personally, I try to steer away from processed foods for breakfast by eating foods that are going to give me sustained energy and

concentration for many hours to come. The way I see it, it's about starting my day with the solid building blocks of nourishment, ingredients that contain plenty of soluble fiber, vitamins and minerals, healthy fats (like omega-3s), and protein to promote long-lasting fullness, energy, and good digestion. So I love to have a rosemary and sweet potato frittata, brown rice porridge (with chia seeds and figs), or quinoa with papaya and honey while sitting down, so I can take my time to enjoy and digest it. If there's one meal I don't mind overindulging in, it's breakfast, because I'll have the whole day to burn it off.

Plus, there's another hidden benefit to having a healthy breakfast: By being conscious of and accountable for your food choices first thing in the morning, you will set yourself up to make better eating decisions throughout the day. By starting off on the right foot, you'll want to continue the delicious, nutritious style of eating that kick-started your day. Trust me: When I begin the morning with a good breakfast, I'm more likely to eat well all day long while keeping my hungry tummy under control. This way, my body gets the good-quality energy it thrives on, my mind is better able to stay focused, and my taste buds are thrilled throughout the day. It's a triple win, really.

GET JUICED

I love starting my day with fresh juice because it provides a great burst of flavor and color and a quick shot of energy. It can be as simple as a big glass of ice-cold orange juice or one of my many fun, creative (alcohol-free) cocktails, made with pretty much anything that's in sight. The crazy thing is, I don't really crave particular flavors as much as I do colors: I have moments where I think, "Well, I haven't eaten enough green food this week," or "I don't remember eating anything red this week!" and I'll create a juice that helps me catch up on the nutrients I've missed from Mother Nature's rainbow. To make juicing more affordable, I tend to buy large quantities of fresh fruit and vegetables in bulk from the grocer or farmers' market; buying local and in-season produce should also help keep costs down.

Below is a list of my favorite go-to juices. I don't really have a set amount of ingredients that go into each juice (though I have provided approximate measures per serving), so the flavor will vary every time. Still, it's good to keep in mind some basic principles: Ginger is a really strong flavor; lemons are sour; beets are earthy in flavor and texture; and apples and pears are super sweet. Use the measurements below as approximate guidelines, but feel free to tinker with the amounts to please your palate. Simply toss the ingredients in a blender or juicer, hit the On button, and have fun creating a nutritious drink that will delight your senses.

Green Juices

Green Eden: 1 apple, 1 medium cucumber, 4 kale leaves, 1 lemon (skin removed), 1 small knob of fresh ginger

The Green Aura: 1 pear, ½ medium cucumber, 3 stalks celery, ½ cup mint leaves; add a 6-inch piece of aloe vera (skin removed and finely diced) and 2 tablespoons chia seeds

Red Juices

Red Dragon: 3 cups cubed watermelon, 1 pear, 1 medium beet, 1 lemon (skin removed)

The Red Garden: 2 tomatoes, 3 medium carrots, 1 medium beet, 2 stalks celery, fresh basil

Orange Juices

Orange Blush: 2 oranges (skin removed), 3 medium carrots, 1 lemon (skin removed), 1 small knob of fresh turmeric (or 1 teaspoon dried turmeric, mixed into the juice)

The Morning Sunshine: ¼ fresh pineapple (skin removed and cubed), 1 orange (skin removed), 2 stalks celery, 2 tablespoons chia seeds

As much as I love my morning juice, I don't rely on it solely to give me the nutritional building blocks to get me through the a.m. After fasting all night, my body is looking for long-sustaining fuel in the form of complex carbohydrates, proteins, and fats. The recipes that follow provide all that, as well as a good dose of fiber to maintain digestive health and boost feelings of fullness.

BIRCHER MUESLI WITH TOASTED COCONUT AND STRAWBERRIES

I love my Bircher muesli, and I find the whole concept of making it the night before very appealing; besides saving time in the morning, it really comes out best this way. I can be at my table, eating breakfast, in a matter of moments. Being able to get up and go for a run or bike ride and come home to a substantial helping of Bircher muesli topped with toasted coconut and fresh strawberries is a great way to celebrate every morning of the year.

SERVES 4

2 cups gluten-free organic rolled oats (Note: When buying oats, if you are gluten intolerant or have celiac disease, be sure to read the package to make sure they're not processed in the same facility as grains that contain gluten.)

⅓ cup toasted sesame seeds

1 cup organic apple juice

1 cup coarsely grated apple

½ cup plain yogurt

Juice of 1 grapefruit

⅓ cup toasted, flaked, unsweetened coconut

1 (6-ounce) basket of strawberries, hulled and quartered

1. Place oats, sesame seeds, and juice in a large bowl and soak for an hour, or preferably overnight.

2. Add grated apple, yogurt, and grapefruit juice to the oat mixture and mix well.

3. Spoon the Bircher muesli into serving bowls and top with coconut and strawberries.

Note: If strawberries are unavailable, banana or mango slices work well, too!

Breakfast Fruits

I think one of my all-time favorite memories of working in a commercial kitchen was when my fruit and vegetable supplier would deliver the first of the season's stone fruits—peaches, nectarines, plums, and apricots—or, in winter, the cooler-climate fruits like pears, apples, quince, and citrus fruits. I was grateful to receive fresh fruits from local farms when they were in season, naturally ripe, and at their flavorsome and textural best. Their fruitful smell would linger in the kitchen, and at times, if I had trays of fruits that needed a couple more days to ripen before they were ready to be poached, pickled, or stewed, I would let them sit out, and their aroma would fill the restaurant in a sublime way.

Poached Stone Fruits

When it comes to poaching peaches, nectarines, or apricots, I prefer to drop the ripe fruit into a pot of boiling water for 20–30 seconds, and then transfer them into ice-cold water to help remove the skin before poaching them. As for plums and cherries, their skin is a little trickier to deal with, so I poach these with the skin on. Cook these as directed above, using the same ingredients (other than the fruits) in the same quantities.

Stewed Fruit

Thanks to its sweet and savory nature, stewed fruit lends itself to breakfast (with yogurt, oatmeal, or granola), dessert toppings, and smoothies. Plus, it's another great way to get more mileage out of your food budget, because you can stew fruits when they've passed their prime. I especially like to stew fruits when the fruit has surpassed that perfectly ripe stage for poaching and it feels a little too soft for either poaching or eating fresh.

Berries, rhubarb, apples, pears, and stone fruits are all great for stewing. It's hard to give the exact quantities because acid levels and sweetness in the fruits will vary considerably, so I'm going to have to give you rough estimates. Ultimately, you'll need to judge the measurements. Remember that tangy fruits will need a little more sugar. Be sure to discard any bruised or bad fruit, because these will taint your final results.

Poached Pears

4 cups cold water

2 cups sugar

Juice and zest of 1 lemon

1 vanilla bean, split lengthways, seeds
scraped and reserved (optional)

6 medium-size pears (Bosc, William, Anjou,
or French Butter, if possible)

1. In a pot that's large enough to hold all the ingredients, place everything except the pears. Stir the mixture until the sugar has almost dissolved before you heat the pot.

2. Peel the pears, leave them whole, and place them into the liquid.

3. Cover the pot with a piece of parchment paper to prevent any moisture loss. Place over medium heat and bring to a boil.

4. Once the pears have reached the boiling point, remove the pot from the heat and allow it to cool. Do not refrigerate it right away, as this could adversely affect the sensuous texture of the pears; once they've cooled to room temperature, you may refrigerate the pears for later use.

Rhubarb

1 bunch rhubarb, green leaves removed,
ends trimmed, cut into 3-inch pieces

½ inch peeled, finely sliced ginger

½ cup brown sugar

½ cup water or orange juice

Place all ingredients into a heavy-bottomed pan and set over a low to moderate heat. Cover the pan with a lid and cook until the rhubarb is softened but not broken up, approximately 10–22 minutes.

Peaches and Strawberries

6 peaches, peeled and stones removed (see
above technique for removing skins)

2–3 cups strawberries, hulled and split in
half

¼ cup sugar

Place all ingredients into a heavy-bottomed pan and set over a low to moderate heat. Cover the pan with a lid and cook until the fruit is softened but not broken up, approximately 10–15 minutes, depending on ripeness of the fruit.

BREAKFAST PARFAIT

A breakfast parfait or sundae is a great way to include a little bit of everything on your fork or spoon in the morning. Similar to Bircher Muesli (page 14), you can make it a day ahead; this way, it makes for a perfect grab-and-go breakfast. Breakfast parfaits are pretty simple to put together, and I like placing these in old-fashioned preserving or canning jars to serve. The only limit to the flavors and textures in the parfait is your own imagination. To simplify this recipe, you could use muesli instead of the quinoa, almonds, and chia seeds.

MAKES 4 SERVINGS

1½ cups cooked quinoa
2 tablespoons chia seeds
½ cup chopped raw almonds
2 cups Greek-style yogurt, divided
1 cup stewed rhubarb (see page 16)
1 cup fresh blueberries
Fresh mint leaves (optional)

1. Mix together the quinoa, chia seeds, and almonds.

2. Place ¼ cup yogurt in the base of each jar or serving vessel, then evenly distribute the quinoa mixture between the jars. Top this with the remaining yogurt followed by the stewed rhubarb.

3. At this point, you can cover the parfaits and leave them in the refrigerator overnight, or you can serve them straight away, topped with fresh blueberries and a little fresh mint, if desired.

This is one of my all-time favorite ways to start the day. If you cook the brown rice in advance, you can quickly assemble the porridge. When it comes to toppings, look to the seasons—choose ripe stone fruits (such as peaches, plums, and nectarines) in the summer and succulent berries, apples, and pears in the cooler months. You could certainly embellish your porridge with a vanilla bean, if budget permits.

SERVES 2

1½ cups cooked brown rice
1½ cups coconut or almond milk
½ cup dried figs, tops removed, split in half
¼ cup chia seeds
2 tablespoons whole almonds, toasted and
   chopped
1 fresh, young coconut, finely sliced
   (optional) (if accessible, use the fresh
   coconut milk to soak the chia seeds)

1. In a small saucepan over medium heat, warm the brown rice with half the coconut or almond milk and the dried figs. Once it's hot, remove it from the heat.

2. Soak the chia seeds in the remaining coconut or almond milk for 10 minutes, or until the chia seeds swell and develop a translucent casing.

3. Fold together the brown rice and the chia seeds, then mix in the chopped almonds and the figs. Top with fresh coconut, if desired, and serve.

BUCKWHEAT CREPES WITH CRÈME FRAÎCHE
AND BLACKBERRIES

Since I became gluten-free, I have mostly steered away from all processed grains. But on the off chance I get a craving for a pancake or a sweet or savory crepe, I don't mind delving into my buckwheat stash. This is a pretty basic recipe, and when it comes to the fillings, you can really go to town. (Just remember to exercise portion control and willpower!) Sweet or savory, these are delicious and easy! If crème fraîche is not available, you could make your own or replace it with something like fresh ricotta or a lightly sweetened yogurt.

MAKES 6 (10-INCH) CREPES

1½ cups water

3 eggs

2 tablespoons unsalted butter, melted, plus more for cooking

1 cup buckwheat flour

½ cup gluten-free all-purpose flour

1 tablespoon sugar

¼ teaspoon salt

1 cup crème fraîche

2 cups blackberries

1. Gently whisk together the water, eggs, and 2 tablespoons melted butter until they're just combined.

2. Add the dry ingredients and whisk the mixture until smooth, then set aside.

3. Place ½ teaspoon butter in a nonstick pan and heat it over medium heat until the butter starts to foam. Pour in enough batter to cover the pan thinly when it's swirled around, and allow it to cook for 25–30 seconds. Flip it over using a spatula and cook for another 10–15 seconds. Repeat until all the crepes are cooked.

4. To serve, place the crepes in the middle of a table and allow everyone to make their own by placing a little crème fraîche and fresh berries on each one.

To make your own crème fraîche, you'll need:

4 cups cream

1½ cups buttermilk

1. Place the cream and buttermilk in a large saucepan over low heat and bring it to 99°F (37°C) when tested with a thermometer. (If you don't have a cooking thermometer, the best way to test is by dipping a clean finger into the cream; it should feel neither warm nor cold.)

2. Pour the mixture into a clean bowl, set it in a warm place (such as near a warm stove or oven), and cover it with a clean towel. After 24 hours, the cream should be somewhat thickened, and there should be a watery substance below the surface. If it hasn't quite set, leave it be for longer.

3. Separate the curds from the whey: Using a ladle, skim the thick cream into a clean bowl or jar, separating as much cream from the whey as possible. (The whey will look like milky water.) Discard the whey and refrigerate the crème fraîche for later use.

GRILLED POLENTA WITH SOFT-BOILED EGG AND PROSCIUTTO

I love polenta because of its versatility: Whether it's soft or firm, it works for me at any time of the day. Wet polenta is well suited to braised meat and vegetable dishes, whereas grilled firm polenta is a great substitute for a bruschetta when it's topped with your favorite ingredients. This recipe is for firm polenta, which I consider a great weekend breakfast or brunch dish.

SERVES 2

2 cups chicken stock or lightly salted water
½ cup fine or instant polenta
2 tablespoons unsalted butter
⅓ cup grated Parmesan
Ground black pepper, to taste
Extra-virgin olive oil
⅓ cup cornstarch, tapioca flour, or rice flour
2 eggs
4 large leaves radicchio, washed and patted
   dry with paper towel
1 teaspoon olive oil
Salt and pepper, to taste
1 teaspoon balsamic vinegar
6 thin prosciutto slices

1. Bring the stock or water to a boil in a medium-size saucepan. Slowly pour in the polenta, whisking it continuously to prevent the polenta from clumping together.

2. Reduce the heat to low and continue cooking the polenta for 12–15 more minutes. When the polenta starts to pull away from the sides of the pan, add the butter, cheese, and black pepper.

3. If you'll be serving it wet or soft, keep the polenta warm until you're ready to serve (if it thickens too much, feel free to add a little more stock to thin it). For firm polenta, pour the mixture onto a plate or tray and spread it out to form a roundish cake, ¾ inch thick, and set it aside to cool for 30 minutes.

4. Once it has cooled, slice the polenta into ½-inch-thick slices, wedges, or triangles. Either brush each piece with a little olive oil and grill them on both sides for a few moments on a hot grill plate, or place the pieces in a heavy-bottomed pan (the polenta will need to be dusted with a little tapioca, corn, or rice flour to prevent sticking), add a little olive oil, and cook the pieces on both sides until they're golden.

5. Prepare the soft-boiled eggs by carefully spooning the eggs into a pot of boiling water and setting a timer for 6–8 minutes. When it goes off, remove the eggs from the pot and place them into a bowl of cold water for 30 seconds. While eggs are cooking, quickly grill the radicchio leaves with a little olive oil, salt, and pepper. Once wilted, remove from grill plate (after approximately 30–40 seconds), sprinkle with the balsamic, and set aside.

6. Gently peel the eggs, cut into halves, and place them alongside the grilled polenta, radicchio, and a few slices of prosciutto. Drizzle with a little extra-virgin olive oil, top with a good crack of fresh black pepper, and serve.

HUEVOS RANCHEROS

This is a great way to start any weekend; the flavors and textures in this portion-controlled breakfast are nothing short of spectacular! This dish is something that takes a little more time than many morning meals, but it produces the *ultimate* breakfast, one that's rich in nutrients, flavors, textures, and colors. Plus, it's a meal that keeps me fueled and satisfied for hours!

SERVES 2

2 large tomatoes, cored and finely diced

½ small red onion, peeled and finely chopped

1 medium jalapeño pepper, seeds removed and finely chopped

1 tablespoon plus ¼ cup olive oil

1 small lime

Salt and freshly ground pepper, to taste

2 cloves garlic, peeled and sliced

1 (15.5-ounce) can black beans, well drained

¼ cup water

¼ teaspoon ground coriander seed

4 (6-inch) corn tortillas

2 eggs

1 avocado, skin and seed removed and roughly diced

¼ bunch fresh cilantro, leaves and stems washed and chopped

1. Preheat the oven to 400°F (205°C).

2. Mix the diced tomatoes, onion, and jalapeño with 1 tablespoon olive oil and a little lime juice. Season with salt and pepper and set the tomato salsa aside.

3. In a heavy-bottomed saucepan, lightly fry the garlic in ¼ cup olive oil over moderate heat without letting it change color, then add the beans. Using a fork, roughly crush the beans; add ¼ cup water along with a good pinch of salt and the ground coriander seed. Cook over low heat until the mixture is warmed through and starts to thicken.

4. In a dry large skillet or smaller 6-inch skillets, toast each corn tortilla on both sides (if you have a stove-top griddle pan, that's even better). Then, in the same skillet, lay down 2 tortillas and spread each evenly with a quarter of the crushed black beans. Top with the remaining tortillas and spoon on the remaining black beans, creating a little well. Crack an egg into the well of each tortilla.

5. Place the skillet into the oven for approximately 6–8 minutes, or until the eggs are cooked to your liking. Remove the skillet from the oven. Serve with the diced avocado, tomato salsa, and cilantro.

MUESLI

When I was growing up, I didn't mind burying my head into various boxed cereals. Now, I would rather eat the box than the processed cereal. The reason: I want my breakfast cereal to sustain me until my next meal, not give me a sugar high and then make me want go back to sleep. With homemade muesli, there is a bit of prep and time involved, but given this dish's health benefits, it's well and truly worth it. Feel free to mix and match grains and dried fruits, using whatever is available to you.

MAKES TEN ½-CUP PORTIONS

2½ cups gluten-free rolled oats
½ cup sunflower seeds
½ cup pumpkin seeds
½ cup slivered almonds
½ cup whole hazelnuts
½ cup maple syrup (alternatively, dilute ¼ cup honey with ¼ cup orange or pineapple juice)
¼ cup sliced dried figs
¼ cup sliced dried apricots
¼ cup dried cranberries or golden raisins
¼ cup chopped crystallized ginger (optional)
¼ cup chia seeds
¼ cup flaxseeds

1. Preheat the oven to 340°F (170°C).

2. Place the oats, sunflower and pumpkin seeds, and the nuts in a large baking dish. Drizzle the maple syrup over the mixture and fold it through evenly with a fork. Place the mixture in the oven and bake until it turns a light golden color, approximately 15–20 minutes, stirring occasionally.

3. Let the mixture cool; then add the dried fruits, the ginger (if using), and the chia and flaxseeds. To serve, top with fresh fruit, yogurt, or milk (regular or Almond Milk, see page 40), if desired.

4. The leftover muesli can be stored in an airtight container and will remain fresh for up to 2 weeks.

POTATO RÖSTI

I love making this potato rösti (aka homemade hash browns). This basic dish lends itself nicely to breakfast, a main meal, or a snack. Plus, it's the perfect blank canvas for your favorite seasoning and spices. Every now and then I will add in a little grated beetroot, zucchini, or carrot for additional flavor and color. My favorite decadent weekend breakfast is potato rösti with the addition of a little chopped dill, smoked salmon, and a soft-boiled egg, finished with a little parsley and caper dressing.

SERVES 4

5 medium Yukon Gold potatoes
Salt and white pepper, to taste
2 tablespoons olive oil
3 tablespoons unsalted butter, chilled and
   finely diced

1. Preheat the oven to 400°F (205°C).

2. Grate the potatoes over a clean kitchen towel. Pull the ends of the towel up to encapsulate the grated potato, and over the sink or a bowl, squeeze as much of the liquid out of the potato as possible. Then, transfer the squeezed-out potato into a clean bowl and season the gratings with salt and pepper.

3. Preheat a nonstick 10- or 12-inch ovenproof pan over a medium heat, add the olive oil and push the potato into the pan. Using the back of a spatula, press the potato down, and lower the heat. Take a small amount of the diced butter and drop it around the edges of the pan to help with coloring the potato. Shake the pan to make sure the potato isn't sticking, then place it into the oven for 10 minutes.

4. Remove the pan from the oven and flip the rösti over onto its other side. I'm a fan of just going for it and throwing the potato into the air to flip it. Option B, which may be safer as well as easier, is to simply invert the potato rösti onto a plate and then slide it back into the pan onto its uncooked side. Add the remaining diced butter along the edges of the potato and place the pan back into the oven for an additional 6–7 minutes, or until the potato is cooked through and golden.

Rösti with Smoked Salmon and Egg
¼ cup olive oil
Juice of ½ lemon
1 tablespoon chopped capers
2 tablespoons chopped fresh flat-leaf parsley
Freshly ground black pepper
8 slices smoked salmon
4 soft-boiled eggs (see page 25)
¼ cup fresh dill, chopped for garnish

1. In a small bowl, mix the olive oil with the lemon juice. Add the chopped capers and parsley along with a good grinding of fresh black pepper.

2. To serve, divide the potato rösti into 4 wedges and top each with a couple slices of smoked salmon, a soft-boiled egg, and then a little of the parsley and caper dressing. Garnish with fresh dill.

QUINOA WITH PAPAYA, ORANGE, AND HONEY

Quinoa is something I have really only embraced in the last year because I just didn't know about it. Though it's usually thought of as a great grain, quinoa is actually a seed that's loaded with protein and pretty much every amino acid known to man. It has the textural appeal of couscous and it's as versatile as rice, but in my opinion it has a much nicer earthy, nutty flavor. Generally, I cook an entire 1-pound bag at a time, as cooked quinoa keeps perfectly well refrigerated in an airtight container. Whether it's for breakfast, lunch, dinner, or as a snack, quinoa lends itself to so many dishes. Feel free to mix and match fruit and nut selections.

MAKES 4 SERVINGS

2 cups water

A pinch of saffron

1 orange or ruby-red grapefruit, peeled and divided into segments, zest finely chopped

1 cup uncooked quinoa

¼ cup raw almonds, roughly chopped

¼ cup pistachio nuts

¼ cup pumpkin seeds (aka pepitas)

½ small ripe papaya

½ cup plain yogurt

Honey

1. Bring 2 cups of water, saffron, and orange or grapefruit zest to a rolling boil in a pot that has a tight-fitting lid. Add the quinoa and bring the water back to a boil. Lower the heat, cover the pot with a lid, and continue to cook the quinoa until all the liquid is absorbed, approximately 10–12 minutes.

2. Remove the pot from the heat, take off the lid, and allow the quinoa to cool. Fluff the cooled quinoa with a fork and add in the almonds, pistachios, and pumpkin seeds.

3. To serve, scoop one-fourth of the quinoa into each of four bowls, top it with pieces of papaya and orange or grapefruit segments, as well as a small dollop of yogurt and a drizzle of honey.

ROSEMARY AND
SWEET POTATO FRITTATA

I love a good frittata because it's another blank canvas for whatever flavors and textures you choose to work with. It's important to note that if you're experimenting, some vegetables release a lot of moisture, so I suggest that you partly cook, then dry them first; I'm talking about things like tomatoes, peppers, and mushrooms, all of which contain a lot of water. This is something you can make during a weekend and then enjoy the leftovers during the week. Stored in the fridge, it'll keep for 3 to 4 days.

SERVES 6

1½ pounds sweet potatoes
2 pounds onions, peeled and finely sliced
3 tablespoons unsalted butter
10 large eggs (if you keep them at room
    temperature, they'll cook more quickly)
Salt and pepper
¼ bunch fresh rosemary, stems removed,
    leaves finely chopped
⅓ cup finely grated Parmesan
6 ounces soft goat cheese, crumbled
A few small basil leaves

1. Preheat the oven to 340°F (170°C).

2. Wrap the sweet potatoes individually in aluminum foil, transfer them to a baking sheet, and place the sheet into the preheated oven. Cook for approximately 35 minutes or until the potatoes are tender and bear very little resistance when they're pierced with a small knife or skewer. Remove them from the oven and allow them to cool while still wrapped in foil. (Leave the oven set at this temperature to cook the frittata once it's assembled.)

3. Once the potatoes have cooled, remove their skin and roughly cut them into ½-inch cubes.

4. Cook the onions in the butter in a saucepan over medium heat until the onions look slightly nutty in color; this could take 20–25 minutes.

5. Crack the eggs into a large bowl, whisk them, and season with salt and pepper.

6. Scatter the cooked and cubed sweet potato along with the onion over the bottom of a heated nonstick, ovenproof pan. Sprinkle the chopped rosemary and grated Parmesan on top. Pour the egg mixture over; the potatoes should be well covered.

7. Bake the dish in the preheated oven for approximately 20–25 minutes or until the eggs are firm to the touch. Remove the dish from the oven and allow it to cool for 10 minutes.

8. Cut the frittata into wedges and top each with a little goat cheese and fresh basil.

SCRAMBLED EGGS WITH FRESH AND ROASTED TOMATO SALAD

As much as I love them, I try not to overindulge in eggs; I limit myself to having eggs maybe three times a week for breakfast. This is a basic recipe I have stuck with over the years, largely because the ingredients are truly a match made in heaven.

SERVES 2

2 medium-size tomatoes, cored and cut into quarters

Salt and freshly ground black pepper, to taste

1 tablespoon olive oil

½ cup cherry tomatoes, cut in half

1 small zucchini, thinly sliced (preferably on a mandoline)

A few fresh basil or tarragon leaves for garnish (optional)

4 eggs

3 tablespoons extra-virgin olive oil

2 tablespoons water

½ teaspoon unsalted butter

1. Preheat the oven to 375°F (190°C).

2. Place the cored and quartered tomatoes into a baking dish, season them with salt, pepper, and a little olive oil, then place the dish into the oven for 20 minutes.

3. Once the tomatoes are roasted, carefully place them into a bowl along with the split cherry tomatoes and sliced zucchini, and sprinkle a little fresh basil or tarragon on top, if desired. Set aside.

4. Use a fork to lightly beat the eggs, olive oil, and a little salt and pepper together along with 2 tablespoons water. Melt the butter in a nonstick pan over a medium heat. Pour in the eggs, allowing them to partially set before using a wooden spoon to pull the eggs back as you tilt the pan forward. The trick here is to be as gentle as possible so that you don't work the eggs too much (and make them rubbery).

5. Repeat the process of pulling the spoon through the eggs until they're almost set, which should only take a couple of minutes. Once they've set, remove the eggs from the pan right away.

6. Divide the eggs between two plates and serve with the warm tomato salad.

BLT WITH AVOCADO

In my opinion, the traditional BLT sandwich is made so much better by the addition of avocado, and even superior with a little sriracha mayonnaise. If you bake your bacon on a wire rack, you'll reduce the fat content—a much healthier way to go than frying your bacon! If you want to be a little more decadent, you could add a fried egg. The additional flavors and textures crank up the appeal of this perennial favorite.

SERVES 2

4 slices bacon

2 tablespoons mayonnaise

A few drops of sriracha sauce or ¼ teaspoon hot smoked paprika (optional)

4 slices Gluten-Free Bread (see page 39)

1 tomato, sliced thickly

2 lettuce leaves (butter lettuce or iceberg lettuce preferred)

1 small avocado, split in half, skin and stone removed, then sliced

1. Preheat oven to 400°F (205°C).

2. Lay the bacon flat on a wire rack placed over an oven tray and bake until it turns golden, approximately 8 minutes. (Alternatively, cook the bacon in a frying pan on the stove, until it's golden on both sides; remove from the heat and drain well on paper towels.)

3. Mix the mayonnaise with a few drops of sriracha sauce or a little hot smoked paprika, if using.

4. Toast the bread either in a toaster or on a griddle plate until medium brown. Spread a little mayonnaise onto 2 pieces of toast and lay the bacon, tomato, and lettuce on each one; place the avocado slices on top and then the remaining piece of toast. Enjoy!

GLUTEN-FREE BREAD

When I first eliminated gluten from my diet, I actually gave up the idea of bread, pasta, pizza, cakes, and cookies. This was partly because commercially available gluten-free alternatives were never quite as satisfying. Having said that, I do get the odd craving for a piece of toast with breakfast, and that's when I turn to my favorite go-to recipe for gluten-free bread. It generally is denser than regular bread, almost cakey in texture, but this will depend on the gluten-free flour that's used; I like the Bob's Red Mill Gluten-Free All-Purpose Baking Flour—it's a mixture of garbanzo bean flour, tapioca starch, potato starch, white sorghum, and fava bean flour.

MAKES 1 LOAF

4 cups gluten-free all-purpose baking flour
½ teaspoon salt
⅓ cup water
1 cup milk
2 tablespoons organic honey
½ ounce dried yeast (2 sachets)
1 tablespoon lemon juice
¼ cup olive oil
2 eggs, lightly beaten

1. Grease an 8-inch loaf pan.

2. Sift the flour into the bottom of a mixing bowl and add the salt; set aside.

3. In a separate bowl, mix the water, milk, and honey together, set over a pot of warm water on the counter and warm the mixture to 98°F (37°C), if you're using a thermometer, or until it feels lukewarm if you dip a clean finger into it.

4. Remove the bowl from over the pot and add the yeast; then mix in the lemon juice, olive oil, and the beaten eggs.

5. Add the wet ingredients to the flour, and use your hand to mix the ingredients together. (Remember that there is no gluten to work through, so it's not quite as labor-intensive as working with regular bread dough.)

6. Shape the dough into a log and place it in the greased loaf pan. Put it in a warm place (such as a linen closet or near a warming oven) and allow the dough to rise; this will take anywhere from 1 to 1½ hours, depending on the temperature.

7. Meanwhile, preheat the oven to 375°F (190°C). When the dough has nearly doubled in size, place the loaf pan into the oven and bake for 45–50 minutes. The bread should be golden, and you should hear a slight knocking sound when you tap on the top of the loaf.

8. Remove from the oven and allow it to set for 5 minutes before turning it out onto a cooling rack.

ALMOND MILK

I love making my own flavored milks. It's super easy to do, and, more important, homemade milks taste delicious. I like to keep it as organic and chemical-free as possible, so using good nuts and chlorine-free water is key. Soaking the nuts overnight is what gives this the great flavor profile, so there really are no shortcuts; just a little forward thinking is required. (*Note:* I use the remaining almond meal in my Energy Balls on page 88).

MAKES APPROXIMATELY 3 CUPS

1 cup raw almonds
2 cups chlorine-free water
2 tablespoons honey
A good pinch of salt
3½ cups chlorine-free water, at room
    temperature, divided

1. Soak the raw almonds overnight in a bowl with 2 cups chlorine-free water.

2. The next morning, drain the water, then blend the soaked almonds, along with the honey, salt, and 1½ cups water in a blender or food processor until a smooth purée is formed; add the remaining water and process.

3. Pass the mixture through cheesecloth, muslin cloth, or a jelly bag to remove the almond meal.

4. Store the almond milk in the refrigerator until you're ready to use it. Place it in a sealed jar, and it will stay fresh for a week.

CHAPTER THREE
THE MIDDAY MUNCH (AKA LUNCH)

We're all creatures of habit, and many of us get stuck eating the same thing day in and day out. So for most of us, lunch equals a sandwich—end of story! I think it's a mistake not to vary your options for lunch, especially if you're having a heavily processed wheat sandwich, a flour tortilla wrap, or a slice (or two or three) of pizza, because these starchy carbs tend to dramatically raise the amount of insulin your pancreas produces, which later causes your blood sugar to crash and you to feel sleepy, lethargic, or just plain dull-witted in the afternoon. That's not what you want to happen during the prime hours of your day! Plus, if you have the same midday meal again and again, you can easily get into a food rut: Your taste buds won't be satisfied, which can leave you vulnerable to excessive nibbling later.

Usually the problem stems from not planning ahead. It's important to think of lunch as a middle-of-the-day opportunity to refuel our bodies and minds with foods that will help sustain our energy and our concentration and stoke our metabolic furnace until the next meal. Preparing a healthy lunch can be easy, whether you use leftovers from the night before or prepare something like a salad or soup with many different colors from nature. The key

is to think about including a good-quality source of protein, a whole grain, healthy fats (such as nuts and seeds), and vegetables. This balanced approach will keep your body properly fueled for the afternoon and help you feel full and satisfied until dinner. That's why I make sure to include protein—usually chicken or fish—in my lunch.

People think they outgrow lunch boxes when they stop going to school. But a lunch box can be your best ally in your quest for healthier eating and better weight management. If you take a lunch box to work with you, or keep it in your car if you're on the go all day, you can load it up with sound nutrition and fuel for the daylight hours ahead—a wholesome lunch, nuts, fruits, and other energy-enhancing nibbles. This way, you'll be less likely to head to a fast-food joint, a convenience store, or the office vending machine when your hunger reaches the ravenous point.

Preparing a lunch is also a smart way to ensure that your midday meal continues to please your taste buds. It's an economical practice—you won't be spending money on take-out or restaurant fare on a daily basis—and a healthier option than eating out. After all, the lunches you get at take-out joints, fast-food places, or sit-down restaurants probably contain a lot more fat, salt, and calories than what you'd prepare at home. Plus the portions can be gargantuan, which can be problematic for your waistline.

So ditch the lunchtime take-out habit and think instead about developing your own optimal "take-in" strategy. Whether you prepare a lunch to be enjoyed at home or you pack one to take with you, you can control the portions and ingredients that go into it. By using delicious fresh produce, lean protein, beans and legumes, whole grains, and nuts and seeds, you can make your midday meal tasty and healthy—and fuel yourself smartly for the rest of the day. Armed with the easy, healthy recipes that follow, you'll be able to reconceptualize the midday meal in a fresher, healthier direction and reinvigorate your lunch break.

CHICKEN AND ALMOND WRAP

This wrap is a perfect item for your lunch box or maybe even a family picnic. The recipe here calls for a chicken salad filling, but you can try making up your own wraps with other meats or sources of protein. There are a few gluten-free wraps on the market, made with either brown rice or corn, but if all else fails you can use the Buckwheat Crepes recipe on page 23 or lettuce leaves as another alternative.

MAKES 6 WRAPS

1 cup mayonnaise

1 tablespoon lemon juice

1 teaspoon paprika

Salt and freshly ground black pepper, to taste

1 whole roasted (regular-size) chicken, bones and skin discarded and flesh roughly chopped

2 stalks celery, trimmed and finely diced

½ cup roughly chopped toasted almonds

3 tablespoons chopped parsley

6 large gluten-free wraps

1. Mix the mayonnaise with the lemon juice and season with paprika, salt, and pepper. Fold in the chopped chicken, celery, almonds, and parsley.

2. Lay a wrap flat on a cutting board and spoon a decent pile of the chicken salad down the center. Roll up the wrap and set aside. Repeat with the remaining wraps.

3. Refrigerate the wraps until you're ready to serve them. I like to roll up each wrap in parchment paper first; this keeps them fresh and self-contained in the fridge.

THE ANYTIME TACO

In my mind, the taco is the ultimate way to use up leftovers. You can simply toast or grill a tortilla shell, then throw on last-night's leftovers or a few of your favorite ingredients. Since I started going gluten-free, a corn tortilla has pretty much become my replacement for a slice of bread. I like to think of it as a blank canvas that I paint on with a variety of delicious elements. Here are some of my top flavor combos for one taco:

A couple of thick avocado slices
¼ cup shredded roasted chicken
Jalapeño pepper, finely chopped—as much heat as you can handle
A couple whole cilantro leaves
¼ lime, squeezed over the taco to finish

1–2 slices smoked salmon
Hard-boiled egg, quartered (use 1 or 2 quarters per taco)
¼ teaspoon capers
A couple each whole parsley and dill leaves

1–2 large grilled scallops
A few shaved raw zucchini slices
¼ cup Celeriac Remoulade (see page 63)
A few dried chili flakes (depending on your palate)
A couple mint leaves
A squeeze of lemon to finish

1 heaping tablespoon Tuna and Chickpea Purée (see page 102)
2–3 thick pieces chorizo, grilled or panfried
A few fresh mint leaves

2–3 thick slices tomato
4–5 tarragon leaves, torn
Half a garlic clove (to rub on the toasted tortilla)
3–4 black or green olives, pits removed, finely chopped
1 thick slice fresh mozzarella

¼ cup sliced or shredded Slow-Roasted Pork Shoulder (see page 159)
1 teaspoon mayonnaise
A few whole flat-leaf parsley leaves
1 heaping tablespoon pickled radish and ginger (see page 119)
1 tablespoon garlic chips (see page 84)

BOILED CHICKEN AND VEGETABLES

This can be such a fun and humble dish with big flavors, providing you cook the chicken with just enough water (or chicken stock) to cover it. It will be a huge success if you are patient with the cooking process and show it some love. For an extra flavor infusion, I recommend serving it with Mustard Fruits (page 199) and Boiled Egg and Parsley Salsa (page 196) on the side.

SERVES 6

1 medium whole chicken (giblets removed), approximately 4 pounds
3 large carrots, peeled and cut into 2-inch lengths
3 stalks of celery, cut into 4-inch lengths
2 onions, peeled and cut into quarters
7 cloves garlic
Water or chicken stock to cover
Salt (approximately 1 teaspoon for every 4 cups of water added; omit if using chicken stock)
1 teaspoon cracked white peppercorns
1 bunch parsley stalks (reserve leaves for Boiled Egg and Parsley Salsa), tied together with butcher's string
Salt
Ground white pepper, to taste
2 cups cooked and drained chickpeas (canned or freshly cooked)

1. In a large saucepan or small stockpot, if available, place the chicken along with the vegetables and garlic. Pour in just enough cold water or chicken broth to submerge the chicken, then add the salt, if using, white peppercorns, and parsley stalks.

2. Place the saucepan over a medium to high heat and bring the liquid to a boil. Lower the heat and continue to cook on a slow simmer for an additional 20 minutes; then turn off the heat and allow the contents of the pan to sit uncovered for 40 minutes to continue the cooking process.

3. Remove the chicken carefully from the pot and place it onto a cutting board. Remove the thigh and leg joint, using a knife to score between the breast and thighs and your (clean) hands to pull the thigh and leg away from the carcass. Repeat with the other leg.

4. Place the carcass on a cutting board, breast side up, and use a sharp knife to score along the center of the breast, filleting each breast from the breastbone. Slice each breast into ¼-inch pieces, cutting against the grain of the meat. Remove any additional meat that was left behind on the carcass and set it aside, keeping it warm.

5. Set the liquid and vegetables back over a moderate heat, and remove the parsley stalks. Reheat to serving temperature but do not let it return to the boiling point; you don't want to overcook the vegetables. Adjust the seasoning if necessary, and add the cooked chickpeas.

6. Serve the chicken separate from the broth and vegetables, along with some Mustard Fruits and Boiled Egg and Parsley Salsa.

BROWN RICE BOWL (BUT IN A BAG!)

This is a fresh take on one of my favorite Korean dishes—bibimbap. It's super tasty and has a little bit of everything in it, and it's a terrific way to use up leftovers. Once you get the hang of it, feel free to put your own twist on it with cooked and shredded meats, vegetables, nuts, or seeds. This is a great dish to prepare ahead of time, and you can certainly have the parcels sitting in the fridge for a few hours before cooking! The recipe here is for four people; however, it is pretty easy to adjust the quantities so you can make more or less. For the bags, I use regular unbleached paper lunch bags—two bags per portion, one placed inside the other. No worries: These are totally safe to put in the oven.

SERVES 4

4 cups cooked brown rice
1 cup frozen peas
3 tablespoons olive oil, divided
2 tablespoons tamari sauce
Cracked black pepper, to taste
1 large zucchini, cut into long batons
2 medium carrots, peeled and cut into
    long batons
4 eggs
1 tablespoon black or white sesame seeds
1½ cups spinach, wilted in a hot pan with 1
    tablespoon hot water and seasoned with
    salt and pepper
1 cup bean sprouts
3 green onions (scallions), finely sliced
¼ cup fried garlic chips (see page 84)
Hot sauce, such as sriracha (optional)
I lemon, cut into quarters

1. Preheat oven to 375°F (190°C).

2. Mix together the brown rice, peas, 2 tablespoons olive oil, tamari, and a little cracked black pepper. Set aside.

3. Blanch the zucchini batons in boiling salted water for 10 seconds; remove them, refresh them in cold water, drain them, then set them aside to dry on paper towels. Blanch the carrot batons in boiling salted water for 30 seconds; remove them, refresh them in cold water, drain them, then set them aside to dry on paper towels.

4. Divide the rice between the four doubled-up bags, creating a little well in the center of each mound of rice. Crack an egg into the well of the rice in each bag.

5. Toss the cooled carrot batons with 1 tablespoon olive oil and the sesame seeds, then place a small pile on the side of each mound of rice, followed by a small pile of zucchini and spinach around the mound.

6. Bring the open edges of the bag together and tie them off with a piece of butcher's string; repeat with all the bags.

7. Place the parcels onto a heatproof tray and slide it into the preheated oven for approximately 15–20 minutes, or until the egg is cooked but the yolk is still somewhat soft. Remove the tray from the oven and gently tear open each bag. Garnish with a few bean sprouts, sliced green onions, and fried garlic. Serve with hot sauce, if desired, and fresh lemon wedges.

CHICKPEA, GREEN BEAN, AND FETA SALAD

This simple salad is absolutely delicious, fresh, and flavorful. The blend of different taste sensations and textures provides a treat in every mouthful. If the beans are tender and you can get ahold of some good-quality feta, this salad will quickly become a favorite friend. The scattering of fried basil not only looks pretty but also adds a wonderful texture to the salad.

SERVES 4

½ pound green beans, ends trimmed

1 clove garlic

4 tablespoons extra-virgin olive oil

2 tablespoons red wine vinegar

Salt and pepper, to taste

3 small French shallots, peeled and finely sliced

1 (14- or 15-ounce) can chickpeas, drained

⅓ bunch fresh mint leaves, torn

½ cup crumbled feta cheese

1 cup fried basil leaves (see page 80)

1. Blanch the green beans in a pot of boiling salted water for 3–4 minutes, or until they're tender, and then refresh them under cold running water. Once they've cooled, drain them on paper towels and set aside.

2. To make the dressing, bruise the garlic in the base of a mixing bowl, rubbing the bowl with the clove, then discard the clove. Add the olive oil and vinegar, season it with a little salt and pepper, add the shallots, and mix well.

3. Add the drained beans, chickpeas, and torn mint leaves to the dressing. Sprinkle in the feta cheese, toss the ingredients lightly, and scatter the salad with fried basil leaves before serving.

CHILLED BUCKWHEAT NOODLES WITH SALMON AND TOASTED NORI

Chilled noodles may not sound like the most appetizing of dishes, but trust me: They are well worth the effort. The noodles can be cooked in advance; just make sure they are refreshed after cooking in plenty of cold running water and then drained well to prevent sticking. This dish tastes as good as it looks. Most supermarkets have an Asian section, where you should be able to find these ingredients.

SERVES 2

6 ounces buckwheat noodles

1 tablespoon olive oil

7 ounces salmon, skin and bones removed

1 sheet of nori*

2 teaspoons sesame oil

½ small English or Lebanese cucumber

3 tablespoons pickled ginger

1 tablespoon black sesame seeds (toasted white seeds would also be fine)

2 tablespoons tamari sauce

6 sprigs fresh cilantro

Fresh lime cut into wedges

*Nori are sheets of seaweed you can find in the Asian section of your supermarket.

1. Preheat oven to 400°F (205°C).

2. Plunge the buckwheat noodles into a pot of boiling salted water and cook until they're soft, approximately 4 minutes.

3. Heat the olive oil in a small but heavy-bottomed saucepan until a blue haze appears in the air over the pan (this colorful bit of smoke indicates the pan is hot enough, without your having to touch it). Place the piece of salmon in the pan and cook for 3–4 minutes, then turn it over and cook to desired doneness. (I prefer the salmon cooked to medium rare, which requires about 7 minutes total, but this varies depending on the thickness of the salmon.) Once it's cooked to the desired doneness, set aside the salmon and allow it to rest for 5 minutes.

4. Prepare the nori by placing it on a baking sheet brushed with 1 teaspoon of the sesame oil and toast in the preheated oven for 5–6 minutes, or until it's crisp. Cool slightly, then crumble it into pieces.

5. Using a vegetable peeler, peel ribbons from the cucumber, discarding the seeded section in the center.

6. To assemble this dish, break the salmon into smaller pieces, toss it through the noodles along with the cucumber, pickled ginger, sesame seeds, toasted nori pieces, remaining sesame oil, and tamari sauce. Serve topped with cilantro sprigs and wedges of lime.

CHINESE CHICKEN SALAD

This simple salad can be knocked out in a matter of moments, and it's full of flavor and color. I love tamari sauce as a seasoning, not only because it's salty and flavorful but also because it's gluten-free (unlike soy sauce). It's a great dish to prepare ahead of time, and because the bulk of the salad is cabbage, it will hold up quite well once it's made.

SERVES 2

1 tablespoon olive oil

2 (5-ounce) skinless, boneless chicken breasts

Salt and pepper, to taste

3 tablespoons mayonnaise

1 tablespoon tamari sauce

1 tablespoon lemon juice

¼ teaspoon dried chili flakes (optional)

1 tablespoon peeled and finely chopped fresh ginger

1½ cups shredded cabbage (red or white)

½ cup grated or shredded carrot

3 green onions (scallions), finely sliced on the angle

½ cup cooked soybeans, removed from their pods

¼ cup toasted, chopped almonds

½ cup chopped cilantro (optional)

½ cup mint, leaves and stems chopped

1 teaspoon black or white sesame seeds

1. In a small frying pan over a medium heat, heat the olive oil. Season the chicken breasts with salt and pepper, place them in the pan, and cook them for 5–7 minutes on each side until they're golden and cooked through. Allow them to rest away from the heat for 5 minutes before slicing or shredding them.

2. In a medium-size bowl, thoroughly mix together the mayonnaise, tamari sauce, and lemon juice. Then add the optional chili flakes and the chopped ginger along with a little salt and pepper.

3. Toss in the shredded chicken, vegetables, almonds, and remaining seasonings, mixing well. Serve the salad in bowls.

GRILLED TUNA WITH QUINOA, SHAVED FENNEL, AND CUCUMBER

This dish reflects the way I like to eat in the warmer months, when I'm busy with work and trying to maintain a more intensive exercise regimen. It's a lighter meal that's full of flavor and nutrients, and it's pretty easy to prepare. Plus, it's a palate-pleasing way to increase your intake of heart-healthy, anti-inflammatory omega-3 fatty acids in your diet.

SERVES 2

1 cup quinoa (Bob's Red Mill Organic Quinoa preferred)

Salt and freshly ground black pepper, to taste

2 (5½-ounce) tuna steaks

Olive oil

1 small bulb baby fennel, finely shaved (preferably on a mandoline)

3 small radishes, shaved thinly

1 small cucumber, peeled, seeded, and diced

1 cup whole flat-leaf parsley

¼ cup fresh dill or tarragon leaves

2 tablespoons extra-virgin olive oil

Juice of ½ lemon

1. Bring 2 cups water to a rolling boil in a pot that has a tight-fitting lid. Add quinoa and bring the water back to a boil. Lower the heat to medium, cover the pot with a lid, and continue to cook the quinoa until all liquid is absorbed, approximately 10–12 minutes. Remove from the heat, remove the lid, and allow the quinoa to cool. Fluff it with a fork and season it with salt and pepper to taste.

2. Brush each tuna steak with a little olive oil and season with salt and pepper.

3. Place the steaks onto a preheated barbecue or griddle pan, and cook for 2–3 minutes on each side, depending on thickness and how you like your tuna cooked. (I prefer mine still pink in the middle.) When they're cooked to your liking, remove the tuna steaks from the heat and allow them to rest for 5 minutes before slicing.

4. Gently toss the cooled quinoa with the fennel, radishes, cucumber, fresh herbs, 2 tablespoons olive oil, lemon juice, and additional salt and pepper if desired. Slice the tuna, gently fold it together with the salad ingredients, and serve.

NANA GOODMAN'S RISSOLIA

When you make and share my nana's pink salad with your family and friends, you will understand the close, caring relationship between my grandmother and my family. This dish is about love and commitment to a tradition. Definitely make it the day before you want to serve it because it gets better with age: The flavors merge, and the textures soften. The real secret to this salad is to chop everything finely into ¼-inch cubes.

SERVES 6

3 large potatoes
2 green apples, peeled and cored
3 hard-boiled eggs, peeled
1 (8-ounce) can cooked and sliced beets
1 red onion, peeled and finely diced
1 large cucumber, split in half lengthways
   and seeded
2 quarter-inch-thick slices cooked ham
1 (15-ounce) can cooked salmon, flaked into
   small pieces using your fingers
1 teaspoon mustard powder
1 teaspoon salt
1 teaspoon sugar
1½ cups sour cream

1. Boil the potatoes (in their skins) in salted water until they're tender, approximately 35 minutes. When the potatoes have cooled, peel away their skins and cut into a ¼-inch dice, then set them aside.

2. Meanwhile, dice the apples, eggs, beets, red onion, cucumber, and cooked ham into ¼-inch cubes. Add the flaked salmon.

3. Mix the mustard powder, salt, and sugar with the sour cream, then combine this dressing with the chopped ingredients.

4. Allow the salad to sit in the refrigerator for a good hour before serving; letting it chill overnight would be even better.

POACHED TUNA WITH ENDIVE, CUCUMBERS, AND AIOLI

During my four-year apprenticeship to become a professional cook, I lived on cans of tuna. To this day, there are times when I will still open a can for a salad if I'm in a rush; then there are times when I want to impress my guests by poaching my own tuna. (If you want to take the shortcut route, feel free to crack open a can as there are some great imported brands to work with.) You could use the same method to poach other oily fish, like salmon, trout, mackerel, or sardines. The court bouillon below is a poaching liquor that should be made well in advance to draw as much flavor from the vegetables and spices as possible.

SERVES 4

½ cup extra-virgin olive oil

2 French shallots, peeled and finely sliced

1 carrot, peeled and finely sliced

1 celery stalk, finely chopped

¾ cup verjuice* or white wine

1 clove garlic, peeled and bruised

1 teaspoon white peppercorns

1 tablespoon salt

1 teaspoon fennel seeds

1 teaspoon coriander seeds

4 (5-ounce) pieces tuna (approximately 1-inch thick), at room temperature

4 ripe tomatoes, cored and cut into quarters

½ cup cherry tomatoes

A few small radishes (larger ones can be cut into quarters)

2 endive heads, bases removed, separated into individual leaves

1 large cucumber, split lengthwise into quarters, seeds removed, cut into batons

4 hard-boiled eggs, cut in half

Aioli (see page 193)

*Verjuice is an unfermented green grape juice that is available in specialty food stores.

1. In a medium-size stainless steel saucepan, place 3½ cups water, olive oil, shallots, carrot slices, chopped celery, verjuice or wine, garlic, peppercorns, salt, fennel seeds, and coriander seeds to make the court bouillon. Set over medium heat and bring to a boil. Once it reaches the boiling point, reduce the heat and simmer for 15 minutes. Turn off the burner and let the bouillon cool.

2. About half an hour before you want to serve this dish, bring the court bouillon back to a boil, remove it from the heat, and drop the tuna into the saucepan, allowing it to cook off the heat. Within 30 minutes, the tuna will have poached through yet still remain a little bit pink in the center. At that point, remove it from the liquid and set it aside.

3. Assemble the remaining ingredients on a platter, place the tuna among them, and serve alongside a bowl of Aioli.

SALAD OF ROASTED BEETS WITH
CELERIAC REMOULADE AND WALNUTS

Hands down, beets are my favorite root vegetable, maybe because they remind me of my grandmother's Rissolia (see page 59), or maybe just because I love their earthy flavor. On my personal hierarchy of root vegetables, beets are followed closely by celeriac (aka celery root) and then parsnips. Mmm . . . winter's bounty! This is a great salad by itself or served alongside a piece of roasted chicken, pork, or even cold cut meats.

SERVES 4

10 small red beetroots
2 tablespoons olive oil
Salt and freshly ground black pepper, to
   taste
1 large bulb celeriac
Juice of 1 lemon
3 tablespoons mayonnaise
1 tablespoon Dijon mustard
½ cup fresh mint leaves, left whole
½ cup toasted walnut halves
1 orange, peeled and divided into segments
Beet chips (optional; see page 84)

1. Preheat the oven to 400°F (205°C).

2. Scrub the beets under cold running water to remove any dirt, then sprinkle with the olive oil and season with salt and pepper. Wrap each beetroot individually in foil and roast them in the oven for about 40 minutes. To test if they're done, push a skewer into the largest of the beets; there should be no resistance. Remove the beets from the oven and let them cool in the foil for 20 minutes. Peel off the skin using your fingertips; this isn't necessary if the beets are scrubbed well. (Warning: Peeling beets can be a messy undertaking, so be careful not to touch anything you don't want to stain until after you've washed your hands well.)

3. Peel the skin from the celeriac bulb and then slice it into rounds approximately ⅛ inch thick. Slice these into thin julienne strips and toss them in the lemon juice to prevent browning. Combine the julienned celeriac with the mayonnaise and mustard, mix well, and allow this to sit at room temperature for 20 minutes.

4. To serve, combine the beets and the celery root, tossing them very gently, then scatter with the mint leaves, walnut halves, and orange segments. Scoop individual portions onto salad plates or into bowls, and scatter the salad with beet chips, if desired.

ROASTED BUTTERNUT SQUASH,
FENNEL, AND LENTIL SALAD

Served at room temperature, this is a great little salad because it's loaded with flavor and texture, and there is definitely room for you to add your own flair (using different pulses, nuts, and leaves, for instance). It's rich in nutrients (like vitamins A and C as well as fiber). Any leftover butternut squash will work nicely on a grilled corn taco shell with a little shaved fennel and sriracha hot sauce.
SERVES 4

½ medium-size butternut squash, peeled and seeds removed

4 tablespoons olive oil, divided

1 teaspoon fennel seeds

¼ teaspoon cracked black pepper, plus more to taste

½ teaspoon dried chili flakes (optional)

Salt, to taste

Juice of ½ lemon

Pepper, to taste

1½ cups cooked lentils

1 small bulb fennel, thinly sliced (I use my Japanese mandoline for this)

¼ cup toasted, roughly chopped almonds

2 cups baby arugula leaves

1. Preheat oven to 400°F (205°C).

2. Dice the squash into large wedges and place them into a bowl. Pour in 2 tablespoons olive oil, spices, and a good sprinkling of salt, gently tossing so the squash is evenly seasoned.

3. Place the squash onto a baking sheet, cover it with parchment paper, and put the sheet into the oven. Bake for approximately 15–20 minutes; the squash should be golden, caramelized, and tender. Remove from the heat and allow it to cool.

4. In a separate bowl, mix the remaining 2 tablespoons olive oil, lemon juice, salt, and pepper, and then gently toss with the lentils, roasted squash, fennel, almonds, and arugula.

SAN CHOY BOW

I love so many Asian flavors and textures, and this dish is no exception. This recipe contains a blend of ground pork and chicken; alternatively, you could use all chicken, all pork, or all beef. (That said, I do prefer the flavor that's derived from using half pork and half chicken.) The addition of shiitake mushrooms, water chestnuts, bean sprouts, and lettuce adds refreshing textural elements and enhances the dish's flavor profile. This can also be served as an appetizer.

SERVES 8 (SMALL ½-CUP PORTIONS)

2 tablespoons olive oil

½ pound ground chicken

½ pound ground pork

2 tablespoons finely chopped fresh ginger

4 French shallots, peeled and finely diced, divided

6 fresh shiitake mushrooms, finely chopped

1 small can (approximately 5.2 ounces) water chestnuts, drained and finely diced

2 cups bean sprouts

½ teaspoon dried chili flakes

3 tablespoons tamari sauce

2 tablespoons gluten-free hoisin sauce

½ cup mint leaves, shredded

1 head lettuce (iceberg, Boston or Bibb, or radicchio), split in half and separated into lettuce cups

1. Heat the oil in a wok or frying pan until it's hot, then add the ground chicken and pork, ginger, and half the shallots. Stir-fry until the mixture has browned.

2. Add the mushrooms, water chestnuts, bean sprouts, and chili, and toss well. Stir in the tamari, hoisin sauce, remaining shallots, and mint, and mix well.

3. Serve in lettuce cups.

THAI FISH SALAD

I have traveled the world pretty extensively, and one of my favorite food destinations is Thailand, where the use of herbs and the balance of flavors always blow my mind. If you can't get your hands on green mango, then green papaya or even sliced lengths of chilled cucumber will do. It's the balance of sweet, sour, and salty flavors that I really want you to experience.

SERVES 2

1 tablespoon olive oil

7 ounces fresh halibut, skin and bones removed (another fish such as tilapia, snapper, or another firm white fleshed fish could be substituted; so could chicken, pork, or beef, if you'd prefer)

Salt and pepper, to taste

1 small red chili pepper, seeded and finely chopped

1 clove garlic

1 tablespoon palm sugar or brown sugar

Juice of 2 limes

1 tablespoon fish sauce

Handful of bean sprouts

2 large red chilies, seeds removed and finely sliced

1 green mango, peeled, sliced, and finely shredded (julienne-style)

½ small bunch mint leaves

½ small bunch cilantro leaves

¼ cup crisp fried garlic chips (see page 84)

1. Heat the olive oil in a medium-size pan until a blue haze appears above the rim of the pan (this colorful bit of smoke indicates the pan is hot enough, without you having to touch it). Season the halibut with salt and pepper, add it to the pan, and cook it at a medium heat until it's golden, about 3–4 minutes; turn it over and cook the other side. The thickness of the fish will determine the cooking time; the best way to determine if it's done is to pierce the fish with a small knife or metal skewer and test for resistance.

2. Add the chopped chili, garlic, and palm or brown sugar to a mortar (or stone bowl) and use the pestle (a club-shaped object) to crush and mix the ingredients into a paste. Add the lime juice and fish sauce and mix thoroughly. Taste it; if the flavors are slightly unbalanced, add a little more chili or palm or brown sugar so the mixture is to your liking. (Alternatively, you can finely chop the garlic, chili, and palm or brown sugar, and mix these together with the lime juice and fish sauce until the palm or brown sugar dissolves.)

3. After the fish has rested for a few minutes, use your fingers to flake it apart and place it into a large mixing bowl, along with the remaining ingredients and dressing. Mix lightly and serve.

BAKED CHICKPEAS WITH TOASTED WALNUTS, ROSEMARY, AND CHILI

A good friend of mine makes the most amazing hummus at his VB3 Restaurant & Bar in Jersey City, and he sprinkles garlic and rosemary-roasted chickpeas on top of it. They are addictive—nearly to die for—and make for a delicious and nourishing snack. Every now and then I will soak a bag of chickpeas overnight and cook them the next day. (If you don't have time for that, canned chickpeas will do.)

MAKES 6 (1-CUP) SERVINGS

4 cups cooked chickpeas, well drained and patted dry
⅓ cup olive oil
4 cloves garlic, peeled and finely sliced
2 large sprigs fresh rosemary, leaves removed from the stems
2 cups walnut halves
½ teaspoon dried chili flakes
Sea salt flakes

1. Preheat the oven to 400°F (205°C).

2. Place the chickpeas onto a baking sheet and combine with olive oil, sliced garlic, and rosemary leaves. Put the sheet into the oven and bake for approximately 35–40 minutes.

3. On a separate tray, toast the walnuts for 12–15 minutes, or until they are golden. (I recommend setting a timer so that you don't overcook them.)

4. Mix the chickpeas, walnuts, and dried chili flakes together, then season with a little sea salt. Serve warm.

5. Once the mix has cooled, store it in an airtight container. It will stay fresh for 3–4 days; I recommend warming it in the oven for 5–10 minutes at 380°F (195°C) before serving.

SPICED CANDIED NUTS

These are a definite go-to snack for me because they're delicious as well as a healthy pick-me-up when I'm on the go. I also love serving these before a dinner party or even nibbling on them when I'm home alone. There is a little time involved in the preparation, and candied sugar can be a bit tricky to handle, so be careful when dealing with the candy part. Don't be afraid of these just because they contain sugar. Remember: Eating healthfully isn't an all-or-nothing proposition. You can enjoy dishes that have sugar and fat—in moderation!

MAKES 6 SMALL SERVINGS

¾ cup granulated sugar

¼ cup water

1 teaspoon whole fennel seeds

1½ teaspoons crushed white peppercorns

1 tablespoon whole coriander seeds

½ teaspoon crushed chili flakes

2 cups mixed nuts (macadamia, almonds, hazelnuts, peanuts, pistachio, pumpkin seeds)

½ teaspoon sea salt flakes

1. Put the sugar and water into a small heavy-bottomed pan, and place it over a medium heat, stirring until the sugar dissolves. Turn up the heat and bring the mixture to a boil; continue to boil it for a few minutes or until the mixture starts to turn amber in color. Then lower the heat and allow the mixture to darken slightly for several moments, but don't let it burn!

2. Remove it from the heat and work quickly as you add the spices, followed by the nuts and salt. Mix the ingredients well and tip them out onto a baking sheet lined with parchment paper (be careful—it is extremely hot!).

3. Allow the nuts to cool slightly, then pull them apart into small clusters while they're still warm. These will stay fresh for a couple of days if stored in an airtight container in a cool place.

FRIED HERBS (BASIL, PARSLEY, ROSEMARY, SAGE)

I love frying herbs, not only because the result looks pretty but also because they taste amazing and have such a light and wonderful texture. As with the root vegetables, don't cook the different herbs together, since they all have varying cooking times.

For 1 cup fresh herb leaves (some stems are more digestible than others, but they all make for a lovely garnish), you will need 1 cup vegetable oil. To fry the herbs, heat the oil in a high-sided saucepan until the oil reaches 340°F (170°C). Carefully drop the herbs into the pan (they will splatter so stand back!). Watch for the bubbles in the oil to get smaller and then eventually disappear (in approximately 10–20 seconds). Remove the fried herbs with a slotted spoon and drain them on paper towels. Season them lightly with sea salt flakes. If you're not going to use them right away, store them in a warm, dry place, such as a pantry, in an airtight container.

RADISH AND FENNEL WITH SEA SALT

We all know how good raw vegetables are for us, but did you realize they taste truly delicious, too? This dish proves it. It's perfect on its own or as a great addition to an antipasto platter. The combination of the slightly spicy and anise flavors is so refreshing and vibrant. (See picture on page 78.)

SERVES 4

8 radishes, washed and tops trimmed
1 medium-size bulb fennel
2 tablespoons lemon juice
Extra-virgin olive oil
Sea salt flakes and fresh, coarsely ground
    black pepper, to taste

1. Score the top of each radish with a cross about ¼ inch deep.

2. Slice the fennel into ¼-inch-thick slices and douse them with the lemon juice.

3. To serve, pour a thin layer of olive oil onto a serving plate, season the oil with sea salt flakes and ground black pepper. Stand the radishes up in the olive oil and arrange the fennel around them.

BAKED KALE CHIPS

I must admit that it took me some time to embrace the idea of baked kale chips. When I cooked them for the first time, I was surprised by how easy they were to make, and how crispy and flavorful they were. Every now and then I will dust them with a little hot smoked paprika and dried chili flakes for a slightly different flavor. Once they've cooled, you can store them for a day or two in an airtight container. If they soften a bit, place them back in the oven for a few moments to recrisp them.

MAKES 4 SERVINGS

1 large bunch kale, large ribs removed and
　　leaves shredded
2 tablespoons olive oil
½ teaspoon sea salt flakes

1. Preheat the oven to 350°F (175°C). Line a baking sheet with parchment paper.

2. Wash the kale well and pat the leaves dry with paper towels as best as you can; then place the kale into a large mixing bowl. Drizzle with the olive oil and sea salt flakes, and mix well.

3. Lay the kale onto the prepared baking sheet and place it in the oven. Bake it for approximately 10–15 minutes, or until the kale starts to darken slightly on the ends. Serve while slightly warm.

PARSNIP, BEET, AND SWEET POTATO CHIPS

Regardless of my twenty-three years' experience with wielding a knife, I find the only way to achieve a perfect slice with root vegetables is to use a Japanese mandoline. It's best to cook each of these vegetable chips separately, because some will cook faster than others due to their sugar and moisture content. Don't be put off by the fact that you'll be frying them in oil: For one thing, it's vegetable oil, not animal fat, which immediately makes these chips healthier. Second, if the oil is at the right temperature, the chips won't absorb a lot of the fat, and when you drain them on paper towels afterward, they'll lose even more of the oil. But that doesn't mean you should chow down: It's best to view these chips as a small treat or a garnish for another dish.

SERVES 4

1 pound root vegetables of your choice
    (parsnips, beets, sweet potatoes, turnips)
4 cups neutral oil for frying (such as canola,
    rice bran, or sunflower)
Sea salt flakes, to taste

1. The best way to get an evenly cooked chip is to blanch the sliced vegetable first in boiling water for 30 seconds; remove it and allow it to dry out on paper towels, separating each slice, so they don't stick together. (Do not refresh or run under cold water.)

2. Fill a large saucepan or wok halfway with oil and heat it to 330°F (165°C). Drop the dry vegetables into the oil, and use a slotted spoon to move the chips around for a few moments. You will notice the bubbles in the oil get smaller as the moisture is cooked out. The chips will be done when the oil nearly stops bubbling and the chips have darkened somewhat and look dried.

3. Remove the chips with a slotted spoon and drain them on paper towels. Season with sea salt flakes, then serve. You can store the leftovers in an airtight container, in a dry place, for up to 2–3 days. To refresh them if they have softened, place them on a baking sheet in a low temp oven (320°F [160°C]) for 10–15 minutes.

Note: Garlic chips can be cooked the same way as the root vegetables, only in smaller quantities. To remove some of the bitterness, and to help the chips color evenly, blanch the thin slices of garlic first: To do this, place them in cold water, bring the water to a boil, then strain the chips immediately. Repeat this process three times before laying the chips out on paper towels to dry.

APPLE CHIPS

I like to use Granny Smiths or Golden Delicious apples for this recipe because of their crisp texture and slightly sweet flavor profile. (Granny Smiths add a touch of tartness, while Golden Delicious apples have a more mellow sweetness.) When choosing apples for these chips, it's best to use older ones that are slightly dry and wrinkly, as these will dry out more quickly in the oven and result in a sweeter chip.

MAKES 4 SERVINGS

2 cups water
1 cup granulated sugar
Juice of 1 lemon
2 Golden Delicious or Granny Smith apples, cored and finely sliced

1. Preheat the oven to 200°F (93°C). Line a baking sheet with parchment paper.

2. In a pot, bring the water, sugar, and lemon juice to a boil. Separate the apple slices and plunge a few at a time into the boiling syrup for 10 seconds; remove them from the syrup and lay them individually onto the parchment paper.

3. Place the baking sheet into the preheated oven and bake for 45 minutes before turning each apple slice over and cooking for another 35–40 minutes (time will vary depending on how thin and dry your apples are to start). The apples will have a dry and somewhat shriveled appearance, but they shouldn't change color much.

4. Once they've cooled, store the chips in an airtight container for up to 3–4 days.

KIWI AND STRAWBERRY CHIPS

Rather than being fried like the vegetable chips, kiwi and strawberry chips are made crisp in the oven. They're perfect for garnishing various dishes and desserts, adding to your own trail mixes, or eating as a simple snack. The drying time in the oven will vary between fruits due to their moisture content; the important thing to remember is that the oven is on a low heat and it's a slow cooking process.

When making this recipe, keep in mind that 1 cup fresh kiwi and strawberry slices will yield ½ cup of the final product. Preheat the oven to 320°F (160°C). Slice the fruit into matchstick-thin slices. Lay the slices flat onto a baking sheet covered with parchment paper and place into the preheated oven for 2–3 hours, flipping the fruit halfway through. The length of time will depend on the natural sugar and moisture levels in the fruit and how thickly you slice them, but the chips will be done when you see shrinkage around the edges of the fruit and a dried-out appearance. Once they've cooled, store the chips in an airtight container for up to 3–4 days.

WALNUT AND FIG ENERGY BARS

I love my energy bars! They are really easy to make and you can play around with different nuts and dried fruits once you get the hang of this recipe. Then you'll always have some sort of snack available when you're craving something sweet. At least with these, you know they're not full of artificial sweeteners and preservatives, and they taste so good. Don't eat them all at once! Share the joy.

MAKES 27 (1 X 3-INCH) BARS

1 cup rolled oats (gluten-free)
1½ cups dried figs
1 cup dried apples
1 cup pitted dates
½ cup chopped walnuts
½ cup raisins
2 tablespoons chia seeds
½ cup orange juice
½ cup toasted sesame seeds

1. Mix all the ingredients, except the orange juice and sesame seeds, together in a large bowl. Process the mixture in three separate batches in a food processor with enough orange juice until the mixture sticks together.

2. Evenly scatter half of the sesame seeds over the base of a 9-inch square pan, then press the bar mixture into the pan using your fingertips to push it into the corners. Once the mixture is evenly distributed in the pan, scatter the remaining sesame seeds over the top, cover with a 9-inch square piece of parchment paper and smooth it over the top of the bars, pushing in the seeds as you go.

3. Place the pan in the refrigerator until the mixture is firm.

4. Cut 3 x 1-inch bars and remove them from the pan. These will stay fresh in an airtight container in the refrigerator for up to 10 days.

ENERGY BALLS

Lately, I've been knocking out lots of different batches of these, especially now that classic cakes and cookies are off-limits due to my gluten sensitivity. Energy Balls are simple to make, and you can play around with different ingredients, flavors, and textures. You can control the texture if you simply pulse your food processor rather than running it on high. If the mixture is a little too wet, try adding a little almond meal or rolled oats to soak up the excess; if the mixture is a little dry, add a bit of liquid.

Bittersweet Espresso Brownie Balls
MAKES APPROXIMATELY 24–28 (⅓-INCH) BALLS

1 cup packed, pitted, soft whole dates

1 cup chilled black coffee

½ cup raw almonds

½ cup raw hazelnuts

¼ cup chopped bittersweet or dark chocolate chips

2 tablespoons unsweetened cocoa powder

2 tablespoons chia seeds

¼ teaspoon sea salt flakes (optional)

½ cup unsweetened cocoa powder

1. Place all the ingredients except the ½ cup cocoa powder into a food processor, and pulse until the mixture comes together. (Don't process it for too long—keep some texture!)

2. Remove the contents from the food processor and transfer it to a bowl; chill in the refrigerator until firm. Once the mixture is firm, roll it into small ⅔-inch balls, then roll and coat these in the cocoa powder.

3. Store in the refrigerator in an airtight container.

Gingerbread Balls

MAKES APPROXIMATELY 24–28 (⅔-INCH) BALLS

1¼ cups packed, pitted, soft whole dates
¼ cup orange juice
½ cup raw almonds
½ cup raw pecans
½ cup rolled oats
¾ teaspoon ground ginger
½ teaspoon ground cinnamon
¼ teaspoon ground cloves
¼ teaspoon sea salt flakes
½ cup almond meal/flour

1. Place all the ingredients, except the ½ cup almond meal/flour, into a food processor, and process until the mixture comes together.

2. Remove the contents from the food processor and transfer it to a bowl; chill it in the refrigerator until the mixture is firm. Once it's firm, roll the mixture into ⅔-inch balls, and then roll and coat the balls in the almond meal/flour.

3. Store in the refrigerator in an airtight container.

Cherry, Pistachio, and Chia Balls

MAKES 22–26 (⅔-INCH) BALLS

½ cup dried pitted dates (3 ounces)
½ cup dried cherries (3 ounces)
¼ cup warm water
2 tablespoons chia seeds
¼ cup raw pistachio nuts
¼ cup raw cashews
½ cup rolled oats
¼ cup dried unsweetened shredded coconut
¼ teaspoon sea salt flakes

1. Place the ingredients in a food processor, and process until the mixture comes together.

2. Remove the contents from the food processor and transfer them to a bowl; chill in the refrigerator until the mixture is firm. Once it's firm, roll the mixture into ⅔-inch balls.

3. Store in an airtight container in the refrigerator.

SMOOTHIES

For me, smoothies are a perfect way to get a quick meal or a substantial snack when I'm on the run. Over time, I have become a lot more creative with them because I keep hearing about new ingredients, some of which seem to come from the depths of some jungle and are supposed to give us strength, wisdom, and longevity. I'm a sucker for claims like that, but I also enjoy doing my own research about them. Here are a few of my favorite smoothies, which contain intriguing ingredients that you may not have heard of (like maca root powder or hemp seeds); you can usually find them at green or organic grocery stores or on the Internet. I prefer to use nondairy milks in my smoothies, and there are some delicious ones on the market, such as soy, rice, almond, hazelnut, and coconut milks.

The following recipes produce a single serving each, but they can easily be doubled or tripled. Hot tip: If bananas happen to be on sale, grab a few extra and when you get home, peel them, cut them into manageable chunks, and freeze them in small containers; toss them into a smoothie instead of ice cubes to give your smoothie a nice, thick texture and an extra flavor boost. With each smoothie, the method is the same: Simply purée the ingredients in an upright blender until they reach a smooth consistency. If the smoothie looks a little too thick, add additional water or milk; if it's a little dull in flavor, add a touch of honey. Then enjoy!

Banana Berry
1 cup almond, rice, or soy milk
6 strawberries
½ ripe banana, peeled (frozen if possible; otherwise, add 6 ice cubes)
1 teaspoon chia seeds

Blue Cacao
1 cup rice milk
½ cup blueberries
½ banana, peeled (frozen if possible; otherwise, add 6 ice cubes)
1 teaspoon raw cacao
1 teaspoon maca root powder

Green Giant

1 cup almond, rice, or soy milk

2 kale leaves

½ green apple (no need to remove the core or peel)

3-inch cucumber piece, unpeeled

½ avocado, peeled

1 kiwi, skin removed

Tropical Bliss

1 cup coconut water

½ cup papaya, seeds and skin removed

4 strawberries

6 ice cubes

½ cup diced pineapple, skin removed

⅓ cup plain Greek yogurt

Figalicious

1 cup almond milk

⅓ cup dried figs, stems removed

2 fresh figs

6 ice cubes

½ cup plain Greek yogurt

1 teaspoon honey

Sticky Date 'n' Ginger

1 cup rice, soy, or almond milk

¼ cup dried, pitted dates

⅓ cup plain Greek yogurt

¼ teaspoon ground ginger

1 teaspoon chia seeds

1 teaspoon maca root powder

½ frozen banana, peeled

SPROUTED
BEANS AND
PULSES

For a long time, I have known about the existence of sprouts and sprouting—as in various types of bean sprouts, alfalfa sprouts, and others— but I didn't know about all the nutritional benefits you can get from eating them. They're loaded with beneficial enzymes, proteins, fiber, essential fatty acids, and vitamins.

To me, sprouted pulses (including beans and lentils) are like eating candy—they are wonderfully sweet, with a crisp, clean texture when you bite into them. Better yet, they are filling and satisfying. A delicious salad of mixed sprouts, with some nuts, diced pear or apple, and little goat cheese can be quite a glorious experience.

MAKES 3 CUPS

2 cups dried white beans, chickpeas, adzuki, or mung beans, green or brown lentils
Juice of ½ lemon

1. Soak the beans in enough water to cover by a factor of two plus the lemon juice overnight, or at least 12 hours.

2. Drain beans well, and then place into a glass jar, cover it with cheesecloth or muslin, secure it with an elastic band in a cool, dry place (such as a windowsill), and watch the magic happen: The beans will sprout shoots at varying times over a 2-day period. I recommend rinsing the sprouts twice a day during this process, returning them to the jar, covering it with muslin, and putting it back in the cool, dry place.

3. Before serving, rinse the sprouts thoroughly under cold running water then drain them well. You can then eat these as a snack, use them as filler in wraps, or toss them into a salad; you can also use them to make a wonderful raw bean/pulse purée.

STRAWBERRY, GINGER, AND HONEY FRUIT JELLIES

These are delicious and pretty easy to make. Once you master the technique, try making your own variations with different fruit purées; the key is to work quickly as the gelatin will set rapidly. I guarantee your kids will not only love eating them but also love helping to make them, too!

MAKES ABOUT 90 (½-INCH) CUBES

1 teaspoon vegetable oil
1 pound fresh strawberries
1½ cups water, at room temperature, divided
2-inch cube of fresh ginger, finely sliced
⅓ cup gelatin powder
½ cup honey
1 cup unsweetened apple or pear juice

1. Lightly grease a 10-inch square baking pan with vegetable oil.

2. Pick through the strawberries, removing any bad or bruised fruit, then place the berries into a blender or food processor and purée them until they're a smooth consistency. For a more refined texture, I recommend passing the puréed berries through a fine mesh sieve to remove the seeds.

3. In a small pot, bring ¾ cup water to a boil with the ginger. Remove the pot from the heat and allow the brew to steep for 5 minutes; strain the ginger from the liquid and reserve the ginger-infused liquid.

4. Whisk the gelatin into the remaining ¾ cup room-temperature water. Once the gelatin has dissolved, whisk in the warm ginger liquid along with the honey, apple juice, and 1½ cups berry purée.

5. Pour the mixture into the prepared baking pan, tap the pan down on a bench or counter to remove any air bubbles, and lay a piece of parchment paper over the top to prevent a skin from forming.

6. Place the pan in the refrigerator for several hours to chill and set. Once the jellies have set, cut them into small cubes and remove them from the pan.

7. Serve at room temperature. These will keep well in an airtight container in the refrigerator for up to 10 days.

TRAIL MIXES

I always have a little bag of trail mix in the back of my cycling jersey for the sake of convenience. There are times when I feel that if it wasn't for a little extra energy boost from my trail mix, I would never finish some of the mammoth rides I do. Besides, making your own trail mix is fun, especially if you get creative with the mixes.

MAKES 8 (½-CUP) SERVINGS

Trail Mix #1

2 cups whole almonds
3 tablespoons tamari sauce
2 tablespoons sesame seeds
½ cup raisins
1 cup roughly chopped dried apples
½ cup sunflower seeds

1. Preheat the oven to 375°F (190°C).

2. Mix the almonds with the tamari sauce and the sesame seeds, then place the nuts onto a baking sheet lined with parchment paper. Place the sheet into the oven and bake for approximately 15–20 minutes, or until they look and smell well roasted and are crunchy when you bite into them (when they're still hot from the oven). Remove the nuts from the oven and allow them to cool.

3. Mix in the raisins, dried apples, and sunflower seeds, and then separate the batch into 8 equal portions, packing them into small bags or plastic containers.

Trail Mix #2

1 cup toasted walnuts
½ cup roughly chopped dried dates
½ cup pumpkin seeds
½ cup dried cranberries
½ cup sunflower seeds
1 cup banana chips

Mix together all the ingredients and then separate into 8 equal portions, packing them into small bags or plastic containers.

Trail Mix #3

1 cup hazelnuts, toasted, skinned and cooled
¾ cup dark chocolate buttons
1 cup roughly chopped dried figs
¾ cup pumpkin seeds (pepitas)
½ cup salted, roasted peanuts

Mix together all the ingredients and then separate into 8 equal portions, packing them into small bags or plastic containers.

POPCORN, PECANS,
AND CRANBERRIES

This is a great, simple snack to have in a small bag that you can take on the go. Having this on hand will keep you from getting what I call *hangry* (hungry and angry) in the midst of a busy day; you can keep your energy level up by snacking on something healthy and delicious.

MAKES 12 (½-CUP) SNACK-SIZE SERVINGS

4 cups popped popcorn

1 cup dried cranberries

1 cup pecan halves

Mix the ingredients together in a bowl and then divide the mix up into 12 small bags or plastic containers.

BUTTERNUT SQUASH SOUP WITH MINT AND WALNUT SALSA

This is an old favorite with a new twist—the addition of the Mint and Walnut Salsa (see page 203 in the sides chapter) takes this humble soup to a new dimension. Its heartiness makes it a perfect choice for the cooler months, but, really, it's a treat all year long. You could certainly double or triple the amount of soup you make and then freeze it in smaller portions (after letting it cool, of course) and use it for last-minute meals at a later date.

SERVES 6

1 large onion, peeled and finely chopped
2 tablespoons olive oil
2.2 pounds (1 kilogram) butternut squash, peeled, seeded, and cut into 1-inch cubes
4 cups chicken stock or a good-quality vegetable stock
Salt and freshly ground black pepper, to taste
Mint and Walnut Salsa (see page 203)
Extra-virgin olive oil

1. In a large saucepan over moderate heat, cook the onion in olive oil until the onion is translucent, not colored, approximately 5 minutes.

2. Add the squash and pour the stock over top. Cover the pan with a lid and simmer for 15–20 minutes, or until the squash has softened.

3. Remove the pan from the heat and allow the squash to cool slightly before puréeing it in a blender. The soup should be thick and velvety; you can add extra stock or water, if necessary.

4. Return the soup to the saucepan and reheat. Season it with salt and pepper.

5. To serve, ladle the soup into warmed bowls or mugs and top with a little of the Mint and Walnut Salsa, and a little extra-virgin olive oil.

BOILED ARTICHOKES WITH TOASTED ALMOND AND LEMON VINAIGRETTE

The artichoke, as far as I am concerned, trumps most vegetables: I love them for their earthy, sweet flavor and texture; I love them cooked or shaved raw into a simple salad of arugula, Parmesan, balsamic vinegar, and olive oil. While they are certainly not the easiest vegetable to prepare, once they hit season in the spring, they are a definite go-to vegetable for me. Don't be wary of artichokes because you're afraid they will be too complicated to cook. This dish showcases a great method for cooking and eating them.

SERVES 4

8 medium artichokes
2 lemons, cut in half
Salt, to taste
½ cup plus 3 tablespoons extra-virgin olive oil, divided
1 tablespoon coriander seeds
1 teaspoon white peppercorns
2 tablespoons lemon juice
Pepper, to taste
½ cup whole blanched almonds, toasted and roughly chopped
⅓ cup chopped flat-leaf parsley

1. To prepare the artichokes, trim and discard all the indigestible outer leaves and fibrous stems. Peel away enough leaves to reveal the pale yellow leaves; the stems can be trimmed and peeled back to reveal their pale flesh. With a small knife cut about two-thirds from the top of each artichoke and remove the hairy-looking choke with a small spoon. Rub each artichoke with lemon juice from one of the halved lemons and then place them in cold water with the juice of the other lemon added to prevent browning.

2. When all the artichokes are prepared, discard the water and place the artichokes into a medium-size pot. Cover the artichokes with enough fresh cold water to submerge them all; add enough salt so the water tastes salty; for every 4 cups of water there should be a good teaspoon of salt. Add ½ cup olive oil along with the spices.

3. Cover the pot with parchment paper and bring the liquid to a boil, then reduce the heat to a bare simmer and cook for another 8–10 minutes. The best way to test for doneness is by pushing a paring knife or skewer into the thickest part of the artichoke to test for resistance; the artichoke should be tender but with a slight firmness because it will continue to cook as it cools in the liquid. Remove the pot from the heat and set aside to cool.

4. Meanwhile, mix together 3 tablespoons extra-virgin olive oil with 2 tablespoons lemon juice and 1 tablespoon poaching liquid from the artichokes. Season the dressing with a little salt and pepper, add the almonds and chopped parsley, and mix well.

5. To serve, dress the artichokes in the toasted almond and lemon vinaigrette.

FRESH EGG ROLLS

Besides being a delicious starter, these are a favorite lunch item of mine because they are relatively quick and super cheap to make. They are truly amazing when eaten warm. Unlike traditional egg rolls that rely on a flour-dough wrapper, these fresh ones actually use a pancake-like wrapper made out of eggs to hold the cabbage and other good-for-you ingredients inside. They're a healthy and delicious gluten-free game changer.

SERVES 4

1 small onion, peeled and finely sliced

1 small knob of ginger, peeled and finely diced or grated

2 tablespoons olive oil, plus more for the pan

2 cups shredded cabbage (red or white)

⅓ cup plus 2 tablespoons water

Salt and pepper, to taste

4 eggs

¼ bunch fresh cilantro

2 green onions (scallions) or shallots, finely sliced on the angle

¼ teaspoon chili flakes

¼ cup crisp fried garlic chips (see page 84)

1. In a small saucepan with a tight-fitting lid, sauté the onion and ginger in the olive oil until they're translucent and fragrant, about 1–2 minutes. Add the cabbage along with ⅓ cup water and cover with a lid. Continue to cook for 5–8 minutes, or until the cabbage is tender. Remove the pan from the heat and season the mixture with a little salt and pepper.

2. Crack the eggs into a small bowl and add a little salt and pepper along with 2 tablespoons water. Beat with a fork until the eggs are well mixed.

3. Heat a little olive oil in an 8- or 10-inch nonstick pan. (If necessary, take a piece of paper towel and dab the pan to make sure the oil is evenly distributed for a good nonstick coating.) When the pan is hot enough for cooking, you should see a slight heat haze coming off the pan, or you can feel the heat when your hand is held 1–2 inches above the pan. Add one-fourth of the egg mixture, swirling the pan while covering the base as you would when making a crepe; place the pan back over the heat and continue to cook until the egg has clearly solidified. Use a spatula to gently flip the egg; you may need to ease the edges away from the pan first so that you don't break the egg during the flip. Repeat with the remaining egg mixture until you have 4 small cooked egg sheets.

4. Lay the cooked egg sheets on a cutting board or clean flat surface. In the center of each sheet, place a couple spoonfuls of the cabbage mixture, followed by a few cilantro leaves, sliced green onions or shallots, a little sprinkling of chili flakes, and crisp fried garlic.

5. Roll up the egg sheets into cylinders and serve immediately.

FRESH SPRING ROLLS

Making these delicious spring rolls is a great way to entertain and use up leftovers! They're best served family-style, where everyone can have fun making their own and eating them right away. (To be honest, they really don't last much longer than a day before they start to dry out and deteriorate.) Most supermarkets stock the rice paper sheets and vermicelli noodles. Experiment and have fun with different flavors and textures; if you can get your hands on fresh Vietnamese mint or shiso leaves (an Asian culinary herb), then add them to the center of the table for a really authentic flavor experience.

MAKES 12 PIECES

2 long red banana chilies, seeded and roughly chopped

1 clove garlic, peeled and finely chopped

½ teaspoon salt

2 tablespoons brown sugar

1½ tablespoons fish sauce

½ cup fresh lime juice (approximately 4–6 limes)

¼ cup roasted and chopped peanuts (optional)

3½ ounces rice vermicelli noodles

2 medium carrots, peeled and cut into long, thin batons

6 green shallots

2 cups fresh bean sprouts

Shredded romaine lettuce

½ small bunch fresh cilantro

½ bunch fresh mint

12 large (10-inch) rice paper sheets

1½ cups leftover roasted chicken, pork, or beef, or cooked shrimp

1 Lebanese cucumber, cut into long batons

1. If you have a mortar and pestle, pound the chilies, garlic, salt, and brown sugar to a paste, then add the fish sauce and lime juice and mix well. (If you don't have a mortar and pestle, chop the garlic and chili very finely and mix with the remaining ingredients.) Add the optional peanuts and set aside until you're ready to use.

2. Place the noodles in a medium-size bowl, cover them with boiling water, and set the bowl aside for 8–10 minutes so the noodles will soften and cool. Drain the noodles and set them aside.

3. For family-style presentation, place a collection of raw ingredients—carrot batons, green shallots, bean sprouts, shredded lettuce, and fresh herbs—in the center of the table along with a large bowl of warm water so everyone can make their own spring rolls.

4. Completely submerge 1 sheet of rice paper at a time in the water until it's soft and pliable (approximately 10–15 seconds). Remove it from the water and place it onto a clean towel to absorb the excess water. Working relatively quickly, lay a piece of chicken, pork, beef,

shrimp, or whatever you have chosen down the center of the rice sheet, leaving a couple of inches at either end. Follow with a few bean sprouts on top of the meat, approximately ¼ cup rice noodles, a piece of cucumber, several carrot batons, shredded lettuce, shallots, and a few of the fresh herbs.

5. Fold the bottom half of the rice sheet over the filling. While holding the roll firmly in place, fold the sides of the sheet toward the center, then press down relatively firmly to hold the folds in place while you roll the ends of the sheet toward the middle. Repeat with the remaining ingredients.

6. If you're making these in advance, separate the rolls with a piece of plastic wrap to prevent them from sticking together, and refrigerate until you're ready to serve.

FRESH FIGS WITH ROQUEFORT

When fresh figs are in season and available, I can't resist this combination of delectable flavors. Figs are a wonderful stand-alone fruit, but when they are paired with blue cheese they become downright heavenly! I used to serve this dish during my time at Bistro Moncur in Sydney whenever big black Genoa figs were available. Their jam-like texture wasn't too dry or too sweet—it was just right.

SERVES 4

8 ripe figs, washed
4 tablespoons verjuice*
4 tablespoons extra-virgin olive oil
Cracked black pepper, to taste
4 ounces Roquefort or Gorgonzola, crumbled
Basil leaves, for garnish (optional)
*Verjuice is an unfermented green grape
   juice. If it isn't available, use fresh lime
   juice.

Split the figs in half from top to bottom and drizzle liberally with the verjuice and olive oil. Season the figs with the cracked black pepper, then scatter the crumbled cheese and optional basil over the figs. Serve immediately.

CHICKEN WINGS

I love making my own wings, not only because they are loaded with flavor and I know they are 100 percent gluten-free but also because I'm left with a delicious chicken broth that I can use for soups, risottos, stews, and more. Whether you fry or bake the wings is entirely up to you; the magic is in the dry Spice Mix. The combined flavors of fennel seed, white pepper, coriander seed, and chili is pure yumminess.

SERVES 4

Spice Mix
1 tablespoon fennel seed
1 tablespoon coriander seed
½ teaspoon dried chili flakes
1 tablespoon salt
1 tablespoon white peppercorns

12 full chicken wings
8 cups cold water
1½ tablespoons salt
1 tablespoon peppercorns, preferably white
3–4 fresh bay leaves, if available (use dried if fresh aren't available)
½ cup tapioca flour or cornstarch
4 cups vegetable oil
Sliced green shallots, peeled
Dried whole chili, cut into small pieces (optional)
1 lemon, quartered

1. To make the Spice Mix, grind the spices with a mortar and pestle or in a spice grinder. Set aside.

2. Place the wings, water, salt, peppercorns, and bay leaves in a medium-size pot, making sure the wings are submerged in water. Cover the pot with parchment paper and bring the liquid to a boil. Simmer for 3–4 minutes and then turn off the heat and allow the liquid to cool (this is almost like poaching) and the wings to cook all the way through.

3. Once the liquid is cool, remove the wings from the poaching liquid and let them dry on a cooling rack—the longer the better. (If you can do it overnight in the fridge, this will mean a drier, crispier skin when you fry or bake the wings.) When the wings have dried, separate each one using a sharp knife to cut through the joint, discarding the tips of the wing.

4. Set aside 1 tablespoon Spice Mix to use as seasoning once the wings are cooked. Mix the remainder with the tapioca flour.

5. Heat the vegetable oil in a high-sided saucepan to 345°F (175°C).

6. Drop the prepared wings into the spiced tapioca flour and toss to coat them. Dust off the excess flour and carefully lower the wings into the hot oil. Do this in small batches so you won't lower the heat too much, allowing the wings to fry evenly. Cook the wings until they're crisp and slightly golden, approximately 8–10 minutes. Remove the wings and set them aside to drain on paper towels.

7. To serve, sprinkle the wings with a little of the remaining Spice Mix, and scatter sliced green shallots and dried chili, and squeeze some lemon juice over them.

This dish is all about eating clean, controlling your portions, and adding a special touch to a meal (perhaps for a special occasion dinner). It will positively sing, providing the ingredients are super fresh, cut neatly and precisely, and seasoned well. Salmon is something you can find in most seafood markets and stores, but if for some reason you find a fresher, more local fish that appeals to you, feel free to make a swap.

SERVES 4

¼ cup sugar

¼ cup white vinegar

1 (2-inch) cube fresh ginger, peeled and cut into fine strips (julienned)

5 medium red radishes, finely sliced (preferably on a mandoline)

¼ cup diced fennel

½ cup finely diced seeded cucumber, skin on

½ teaspoon finely grated orange zest

¼ teaspoon horseradish purée (if you can find fresh horseradish, go for it!)

1 teaspoon tamari sauce

Cracked black pepper, to taste

3 heads Belgian endive

10½ ounces sashimi-grade wild salmon, cut into ¼-inch cubes

Sea salt flakes, to taste

⅓ cup crispy fried shallots (optional; see page 198)

1. In a small saucepan, bring the sugar and vinegar to a boil, drop in the ginger, and simmer for a couple of minutes until the ginger looks somewhat translucent; remove the pan from the heat. Add the sliced radishes, cover the pan with a lid, and set it aside to cool.

2. In a small bowl, mix together the diced fennel and cucumber, add the orange zest, horseradish purée, tamari, and a couple of tablespoons of the ginger-radish liquid. Season with a little cracked black pepper.

3. Remove the base of the endive and separate the leaves, discarding any bruised or damaged leaves and keeping the smaller leaves for future salads.

4. Mix the diced salmon with the cucumber-fennel dressing and a little sea salt.

5. Place a good tablespoon full of the salmon into each endive leaf, top it with a little of the drained pickled radish and ginger, followed by the optional fried shallots. Serve at once.

MUSSEL, FENNEL, AND
CORN CHOWDER

I love the beautiful silky texture of a good chowder, which is generally derived from the use of flour (which contains gluten). Fortunately, I have found a way of achieving a very similar texture through the use of cornstarch and potatoes. A little cream to finish will also give you that comforting texture that good chowder is typically known for. If you want to take this to another level, add a little splash of Pernod—I love the aniseed flavor it offers!

MAKES 6 SERVINGS

2.2 pounds (1 kilogram) mussels, cleaned and bearded

3 ears fresh corn

1 tablespoon unsalted butter

2 tablespoons olive oil

1 large fennel head, finely diced (reserve the fennel fronds for garnish, if available)

1 large potato (Yukon Gold, russet, Désirée, or Pontiac), peeled and finely diced

3 cups boiling chicken stock

3 tablespoons cornstarch

⅓ cup cold water

½ cup cream, plus extra for serving

Salt and freshly ground black pepper, to taste

Extra-virgin olive oil

1. Put the mussels in a heavy skillet with a tight-fitting lid, and place the skillet over medium to high heat, shaking the pan every now and then. The mussels will start to open slowly; as they do, remove them from the pan and set them aside. Once they are all open, strain and reserve the mussel juice.

2. Separate the mussel meat from the shells, discarding the shells (unless you want to reserve a couple for presentation). Roughly chop the remaining mussel meat.

3. Remove the corn kernels from the cob. I find the easiest way to do this is to remove the husk and silk and then hold the whole ear flat down on a cutting board; using a chef's knife, cut the corn away from the cob in large shards, rolling the corn against the board as you go.

4. In a heavy-bottomed saucepan over a medium heat, melt the butter with the olive oil. Add the corn kernels, fennel, and potato and sauté for a few moments to release the flavors. Then add the chicken stock and the reserved mussel liquid, and cook for 15–20 minutes, or until the potato has softened.

5. Mix the cornstarch with cold water and then add this into the soup. Bring the soup to a boil and continue to cook it for a few moments; the soup should take on a thick, velvety texture. Add the cream, and season with salt and pepper. Drop in the chopped mussel meat and allow the soup to sit for several minutes before serving.

6. To serve, pour the soup into bowls and top with a little fresh cream, extra-virgin olive oil, optional fennel fronds, and ground black pepper.

ROASTED LITTLE
VEGETABLE SALAD

This dish is based on a day at a farmers' market and all the baby vegetables and other fun ingredients that I found there. If you can't find baby vegetables but you like the idea of this dish, cut larger vegetables into similar-size pieces so you can roast them together. The ingredients list alone tells you that you'll be eating a rainbow of colors, which means you'll be getting a full spectrum of vital nutrients.

MAKES 4 SMALL PORTIONS

1 bunch baby carrots
1 cup small potatoes
2 tablespoons olive oil
8 small onions, peeled
1 bunch medium beets (about 4), scrubbed
   and free of dirt
1 fresh garlic bulb, cut in half horizontally
Salt and cracked black pepper, to taste
Handful of fresh green beans, trimmed
Mayonnaise (see page 195)

1. Preheat oven to 400°F (205°C).

2. Scrub the carrots and potatoes under cold running water, then pat them dry with a paper towel.

3. In a large ovenproof frying pan or skillet, heat the olive oil, along with the carrots, potatoes, onions, beets, and garlic, over medium heat on the stove top until they start to brown a little. Season the vegetables with salt and pepper and place the skillet into the oven for approximately 20–25 minutes, or until the veggies are tender.

4. Meanwhile, plunge the green beans into a pot of boiling salted water for about 3–4 minutes, or until the beans are tender. Remove the beans from the heat and run them under cold water to stop the cooking process. Drain the beans and set them on paper towels to dry.

5. Arrange the cooked vegetables on a small plate and serve with a little fresh Mayonnaise.

SARDINES WITH BOILED EGG,
SPANISH ONION, AND CAPERS

Sometimes it's nice just to compose a plate to share. Not unlike an antipasto, this starter, to be shared among friends and family, is super easy and convenient to put together. Since I became gluten-free, I have taken the pressure off myself when it comes to entertaining by preparing more dishes like this. Good ingredients really do make the difference!

SERVES 2

1 small can good-quality sardines, preferably in olive oil

2 boiled eggs (into boiling water for 7 minutes and then refresh under cold water)

½ small red onion, peeled and sliced into rings

2 tablespoons capers, rinsed and drained of brine or salt

1 cup whole flat-leaf parsley leaves

1 lemon, cut in half

1 head of Boston, Bibb, or radicchio lettuce, base removed, separated into leaves, rinsed, and dried

Cracked black pepper, to taste

Assemble all the ingredients onto a plate and serve. This is designed to be a pick-and-choose-your-own-adventure dish!

THAI CHICKEN POPS WITH CHILI CARAMEL

To me, chicken wings and drumsticks are perfect tailgating food—they're cheap and cheerful. If you have the time, try preparing these the day before for a really crispy, dry skin. Cooking the chicken legs in the salted water (brine) just increases the flavor profile. To turn this delicious starter into a meal, serve with a helping of rice.

SERVES 4

8 chicken legs

8 cups cold water

1½ tablespoons salt

1 teaspoon white peppercorns

1 teaspoon coriander seeds

3 cloves crushed garlic

3 strips lemon peel

Chili Caramel Sauce

½ cup water, divided

1 cup brown sugar

1 (2-inch) cube fresh ginger, peeled and cut into fine strips (julienned)

4 small red chilies, seeds removed and chopped (or ½ teaspoon dried chili flakes)

¼ cup fish sauce

¼ cup fresh lime juice

To Cook and Serve

4 cups vegetable oil

½ cup tapioca flour or cornstarch

1 large Lebanese cucumber, peeled, seeded, and cut into spears

¼ bunch fresh cilantro

2 tablespoons chopped, toasted peanuts

1. Place the first seven ingredients in a medium-size pot, making sure the legs are all submerged. Cover the pot with parchment paper and bring the liquid to a boil. Simmer for 6–7 minutes and then turn off the heat and allow the contents to cool (this technique is similar to poaching) so the legs cook all the way through.

2. Once the legs have cooled, remove them from the pot and allow them to dry on a wire rack in the fridge—the longer the better, allowing for a dryer, crispier skin when you're frying or baking them.

3. Meanwhile, make the Chili Caramel Sauce. Place ¼ cup water along with the brown sugar into a small saucepan, set it over medium heat, and bring it to a boil. Continue to cook the brown sugar until it caramelizes (it should turn a dark amber color, but not burn); add the ginger, chilies, and the remaining ¼ cup water and continue to stir it over a slightly reduced heat for a few moments to stop the sauce from solidifying.

4. Remove the sauce from the heat and add the fish sauce and lime juice; continue to stir for another minute. Set aside and keep warm until ready to use.

5. Once you're ready to fry or bake the legs, take each drumstick and run a small knife just under the cooked muscle of the drumstick, lightly scoring to the bone, scraping away the tendon, and trimming the knuckle (this is called *frenching* the bone).

6. Heat the vegetable oil in a high-sided saucepan to 345°F (175°C).

7. Drop the prepared drumsticks into the tapioca flour and toss them to coat, dusting off the excess starch.

8. Carefully lower the drumsticks into the hot oil, doing so in batches to avoid lowering the heat too much. Fry the drumsticks

evenly, until crisp and slightly golden, approximately 8–10 minutes. Remove the drumsticks from the oil and let them drain on paper towels.

9. Place the drumsticks in a bowl and coat them with the Chili Caramel Sauce. Garnish with cucumber, cilantro, and chopped peanuts, and serve.

WHITE BEAN AND OLIVE SOUP

This is a great soup for the cooler months; it's super rich and tasty. Be sure to make plenty so you can freeze it for convenience (just be sure to chill it well before putting it into the freezer). This recipe calls for soaking the dried beans overnight, which may sound like a hassle, but it's easily done with a little preplanning, and it's a great way to stretch your budget. The addition of a cooked turkey neck or smoked pork hock is a welcome option for additional flavor; just be sure to remove it before puréeing.
SERVES 8

3 cups dried cannellini beans or other white
    beans, soaked in 8 cups water overnight
3 medium onions, peeled and sliced
7 cloves garlic, peeled and sliced
½ bunch fresh thyme
2 bay leaves (fresh, if available)
½ cup olive oil
4 cups chicken stock
Salt and freshly ground white pepper, to taste
¼ cup Tapenade (see page 191)

1. Drain the soaked beans of all water.

2. In a medium-size stockpot over a gentle heat, sauté the onions, garlic, thyme, and bay leaves in the olive oil until the onions soften and become translucent. Add the drained beans and chicken stock; bring to a boil and then lower to a simmer. Continue to cook until the beans are soft, approximately 40–50 minutes. If you feel the beans start to look a bit dry, add a little extra water and continue to cook until they are soft and have lost their chalky texture.

3. Remove the pan from the heat and season the beans with salt and pepper. Allow the soup to cool to room temperature before removing the thyme sprigs and bay leaves.

4. Place the soup into a food processor and purée until it's smooth. Adjust the seasonings to your liking.

5. Serve in a bowl, topped with a little of the olive Tapenade.

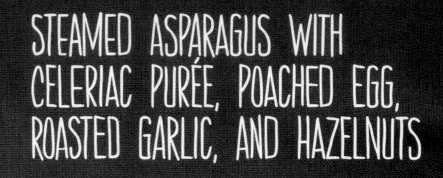

STEAMED ASPARAGUS WITH CELERIAC PURÉE, POACHED EGG, ROASTED GARLIC, AND HAZELNUTS

Not only is this a quick dish to knock out but also the flavor and texture combination is one of my absolute favorites. My good friend Kane (aka the Legend) taught me this method of poaching eggs; with this technique, I get perfect eggs every time. But if you feel this process is too much, then just soft boil them instead.

SERVES 2

1 small bulb celeriac
2 cups whole milk
Salt and pepper, to taste
1 tablespoon hazelnut oil, divided
2 whole eggs
12 medium asparagus stalks , trimmed and
    peeled
10 roasted hazelnuts, chopped
Whole Roasted Garlic (see page 204)
1 small piece Parmesan

1. Remove the thick husk from the celeriac and discard it, then dice the remaining celeriac finely. Place it into a small saucepan and cover it with the 2 cups milk. Bring the liquid to a boil, then lower the heat and simmer the celeriac until it's tender when tested with a small knife or skewer, about 12–15 minutes. Allow the celeriac to cool slightly before straining away the milk, reserving one-third of it.

2. Place the celeriac into a blender and purée, adding a little of the reserved milk until a smooth, velvety consistency is reached. Season the purée well with salt and pepper; keep it warm and set it aside.

3. Take a doubled square piece of plastic wrap and lay it over a small bowl. Drop 1 teaspoon hazelnut oil onto the plastic wrap, followed by a little salt and pepper; crack one egg, being careful not to break the yolk, onto the plastic wrap. Bring the corners of the plastic together, twisting the plastic around at the top, removing as much air as possible, and tie in a knot. Repeat the process for the remaining egg.

4. Bring a small pot of water to a rolling boil, then drop the eggs (wrapped in the plastic) into the water (don't worry—the plastic won't melt in the water) and set a timer for 4½ minutes; when the timer goes off, drop in the asparagus and set the timer for another 1½ minutes. When the timer goes off again, remove both the asparagus and the eggs and set them aside.

5. To serve, place a large spoonful of the celeriac purée on the bottom of two plates. Divide the asparagus between both plates. Very carefully snip the plastic around each egg with a pair of scissors and gently ease the egg on top of the asparagus. Scatter with chopped hazelnuts and cloves of roasted garlic. With a fine grater or a Microplane, grate the Parmesan on top and serve.

BEEF HOT POT WITH TURNIPS AND MINT

I get so much joy out of taking a tough old piece of meat and turning it into something special. It's not just because this approach is budget friendly; it also reminds me of my strong roots in French peasant cookery. This dish could easily translate into a Crock-Pot recipe following the same method; it may take an additional hour to an hour and a half of cooking. To complete this as a meal, I suggest serving it with soft polenta or boiled potatoes.

SERVES 4

2½ pounds braising beef (I suggest oyster blade, chuck, or shin)
Salt and freshly ground black pepper, to taste
¼ cup olive oil
⅓ cup brandy
2 medium onions, peeled and quartered
2 large tomatoes, blanched, skinned, and quartered
2 cloves garlic, peeled
2 medium carrots, peeled and cut into large cubes
2 cups red wine (Pinot Noir)
6 cups beef stock
1 tablespoon unsalted butter
1 tablespoon sugar
4 medium-size turnips, peeled and cut into bite-size wedges
2 tablespoons red wine vinegar
1 cup fresh mint leaves, torn
3 tablespoons chopped flat-leaf parsley

1. Preheat the oven to 285°F (140°C).

2. Trim the beef of any visible fat and cut it into large 1-inch cubes. Leave any sinew, as this will break down and become very gelatinous in the slow braising process. Lightly season the beef cubes with salt and pepper and brown them in a heavy-bottomed ovenproof braising pan, using the olive oil.

3. When the meat is brown on all sides, deglaze the pan with the brandy; be careful, as it is likely to ignite. When the alcohol has reduced, add the onions and tomatoes. Add the whole cloves of garlic, carrots, red wine, and enough stock to cover the meat; bring it to a boil.

4. Turn off the heat and seal the braising pan with a lid or some parchment paper to stop moisture from being lost. Place the pan into the preheated oven for 1½–2 hours.

5. Meanwhile, place the butter and sugar in a small frying pan over moderate heat, then toss in the turnips, moving the pan as they start to brown. Once they have caramelized evenly on all sides, you can deglaze the pan with the red wine vinegar and then set aside.

6. After an hour of braising the meat, add the caramelized turnips to the braising pot and continue to cook until the meat has very little resistance when it's pierced with a skewer or small knife. Once it's fully cooked, add the mint leaves and allow it to rest for a good 20 minutes.

7. Use a ladle to skim away any visible fat from the cooking liquid. The best way to serve this is to finish with salt and pepper, chopped fresh parsley, and a helping of soft polenta or boiled potatoes.

CAULIFLOWER, CHICKPEA, AND SPINACH CURRY

The ingredients list for this sumptuous, fragrant curry may look long-winded, but the effort involved pays off with every mouthful of the final product. Not only is this dish low in fat, but also it's packed with nutritional goodness and satisfying flavors. It keeps well and tastes even better the day after it is cooked. So it's definitely worth making when you have a bit of extra time so that you can then enjoy quick leftovers throughout the week. (For the meat lovers in your life, you can add ½ pound fish or chicken and cook it in the curry.)

SERVES 6

1 red onion, peeled and finely diced
1 bunch fresh cilantro, leaves picked, roots washed, and all finely chopped
1 knob of ginger, peeled and finely chopped
2 tablespoons olive oil
1 tablespoon fennel seeds
1 teaspoon crushed coriander seeds
1 teaspoon ground cumin seeds
1 teaspoon ground turmeric
1 tablespoon mustard seeds
⅓ teaspoon ground chili flakes (if you like your curries hot, add a little more)
2 medium carrots, peeled and cut into ⅓-inch cubes
3 stalks celery, cut into ⅓-inch cubes
1 large head cauliflower, cut into florets
1 (12-ounce) can light coconut milk
1 (12-ounce) can crushed tomatoes
3 teaspoons white wine vinegar
1½ cups water, divided
1 bunch chard, washed and shredded
1 (15-ounce) can chickpeas, well drained
Salt and freshly ground black pepper to taste
Steamed rice

1. In a heavy-bottomed saucepan, sauté the onion, cilantro roots (reserve the leaves), and ginger in olive oil over a medium heat until the onions are translucent, about 2–3 minutes. Add all the dry spices and stir until the mixture is fragrant, approximately 1–2 minutes.

2. Lower the heat and add the carrot, celery, and cauliflower, along with the coconut milk, tomatoes, vinegar, and 1 cup water. Simmer for 20–25 minutes, until the vegetables are tender but still have a slight bite to them.

3. Place the chard into a medium-size saucepan along with the remaining ½ cup water and bring it to a boil with the lid on. Simmer for 2 more minutes, then remove the pan from the heat and let it steam (with the lid on) for another 3 minutes. Add the chard to the curry along with the chickpeas.

4. Before serving, throw in a small handful of roughly chopped cilantro leaves. Adjust the seasoning with a little salt and pepper. Serve with steamed rice.

FISH IN A
BAG

Cooking in a parchment paper bag is a method that has been around for a very long time—and one that I think is definitely underused. Once you have mastered this technique, there are so many ingredients that lend themselves to being cooked in the same manner. This is a delicious way to prepare fish—a healthy low-fat source of protein—with minimal effort and incredible flavor. Cooking in a bag is easy and convenient, and it makes the cleanup a breeze.

Now, I realize that not everyone can appreciate a whole fish, especially one that is looking right back at you, but once you can get over this discomfort, you will appreciate how much more flavorful and juicy fish is when it's cooked on the bone; however, a single fillet of fish can be cooked the same way, though the cooking time will be less, and you will lose a little more of the moisture content.

SERVES 2

8 small steamed potatoes, sliced into smaller rounds
3 tablespoons chopped green shallots
Salt and freshly ground white pepper to taste
1 (1½-pound) whole black bass, snapper, or other firm white-fleshed fish, scaled and gutted
8 sprigs fresh thyme
1 lemon, cut into quarters, divided
3 tablespoons olive oil, divided
1 small zucchini, finely sliced
1 cup whole fresh mint leaves
½ bunch chives, finely sliced

1. Preheat the oven to 395°F (200°C).

2. Lay a large piece of parchment paper (about twice the length of the fish) on a counter or table. In the center of the paper lay the steamed potato slices, sprinkle with the green shallots, and season them with a little salt and pepper. Stuff the fish with the fresh thyme and then put the fish on top of the potato slices. Squeeze a little of the lemon juice over, along with 1 tablespoon olive oil, then season with salt and pepper.

3. To create a bag: Take the edge of the parchment paper closest to you and the opposite edge, and bring them together above the fish; fold the edges downward, creating a tight pleat, then fold the right and left ends back under the fish to create a snug parcel. Use butcher's string to tie the bag and prevent it from opening during the cooking process.

4. Place the parcel onto a heatproof tray, then into the preheated oven for 14–16 minutes, or until the fish is cooked. The best way to test it is to open the bag and pierce the fish with a sharp skewer; you are looking for very little to no resistance. Once the fish is cooked, remove it from the oven and allow it to rest for several minutes before opening the bag.

5. Meanwhile, in a medium-size bowl, mix together the sliced zucchini along with the mint leaves and a scattering of the chives. Season them with a little salt and pepper, the remaining oil, and another squeeze of lemon juice.

6. To serve the fish, tear open the bag, and place the zucchini and mint salad evenly on top of each piece of fish.

FISH PIE

I love a good fish pie. To me it's the ultimate comfort food, not to mention a one-pan wonder! The important thing to remember is that the fish needs to be super fresh and boneless; otherwise, this dish won't turn out the way it should. This is a perfect midweek meal and another great way to get more heart-healthy omega-3 fatty acids into your diet.

SERVES 6

1½ pounds large Yukon Gold or other mashing potatoes, peeled and cut into chunks
5 tablespoons butter, divided (3 tablespoons cubed plus 2 tablespoons)
3 tablespoons extra-virgin olive oil
1 cup milk, heated to simmering
Salt and freshly ground white pepper to taste
Pinch of nutmeg
1 large leek, trimmed of dark leaves, well rinsed under running water to remove any dirt, and finely sliced into rounds (approximately 2 cups)
2 fresh bay leaves (if available, otherwise dried will do)
2 heaping tablespoons cornstarch
⅓ cup cold water
¾ pound fresh tilapia, snapper, bass, whiting, or other firm white-fleshed fish, skin and pin bones removed, cut into large bite-size chunks
¾ pound salmon, prepared in the same manner as above
1 cup frozen peas
½ cup chopped flat-leaf parsley

1. Place the potatoes in a saucepan and cover them with cold water. Bring the water to a boil, lower the heat to a simmer, and continue to cook the potatoes until they're tender, about 25 minutes. Drain the potatoes and return them to the saucepan.

2. Place the potatoes over a medium-high heat, shaking the pan to remove excess moisture. (The time will vary depending on how wet the potatoes are, but this should last no more than a couple minutes.) Then, take the pan off the heat and mash the potatoes until they're smooth, using a masher, or push the potatoes through a ricer or mouli into a bowl.

3. Beat in the 3 tablespoons cubed butter, oil, and milk until the mixture is smooth and thoroughly mixed. Season with salt, white pepper, and nutmeg, and set it aside.

4. In a large saucepan sauté the leeks and bay leaves in the remaining 2 tablespoons butter over moderate to low heat until they're tender but haven't changed color.

5. Meanwhile, mix the cornstarch and ⅓ cup cold water and add this to the leeks, stirring until the mixture becomes thick. Continue to cook it for another 2–3 minutes, stirring frequently to prevent sticking or clumping.

6. Add the fish chunks along with the peas, and bring the mixture to a boil, then remove it from the heat immediately. Stir in the chopped parsley and combine well.

7. Preheat the broiler. Then, lay the fish into the base of an ovenproof baking dish

(approximately 10 inches in diameter) and carefully top the fish with the mashed potatoes. Use a fork to create your own pattern in the mashed potatoes. Place the dish into the oven and broil it for approximately 10–15 minutes, until it's golden and crispy on top.

8. I like to serve this with a little side salad of greens and radishes.

Note: If you're preparing this in advance, it will take a little longer to heat up in step 7 if it's going from the refrigerator to the oven. In that case, I recommend preheating the oven to 375°F (190°C), then baking the pie for 35–40 minutes, or until it's heated through and golden on top.

LAMB CUTLETS IN THE NICE-EAN STYLE

This is one of those quick and easy meals that's packed with flavor and guaranteed to become your new best friend at dinnertime. Every once in a while, I swap lamb cutlets for thinly sliced beef fillet or roasted chicken legs—this recipe really is that flexible and easy. Don't be put off by the anchovies! The flavor that's derived from them is more of a salty complexity than that of a bad pizza.

SERVES 2

2 ripe tomatoes
½ pound green beans
6 lamb cutlets (approximately 4 ounces each)
Salt and pepper to taste
2 tablespoons olive oil
1 tablespoon unsalted butter
4 cloves garlic, peeled and finely sliced
6 anchovy fillets, finely chopped
¼ cup small black olives, pitted (or larger ones that have been pitted and chopped)
4 tablespoons chopped flat-leaf parsley

1. Bring a pot of water to a rolling boil, then drop the tomatoes into the water for 20–30 seconds. Remove the tomatoes (saving the water) and plunge them immediately into a bowl of cold water. Peel off the skin and chop the tomatoes.

2. Drop the beans into the boiling water for 2–3 minutes until they're tender, then remove them with a slotted spoon and plunge them immediately into the cold water.

3. Season the lamb cutlets with salt and pepper, and place them into a preheated heavy-bottomed pan with olive oil and butter. Brown the cutlets for 2–3 minutes, then turn them over and repeat on the other side. (I like to cook my cutlets until they're medium rare; then, I remove them from the pan to rest for another 3 minutes before serving.)

4. To the same pan, add the garlic and anchovies, and cook until the garlic starts to brown and the anchovies dissolve. After about 30 seconds, add the chopped tomato, beans, chopped olives, and parsley. Add the lamb cutlets, gently toss, and serve them with Baked Sweet Potato Fries (page 171).

QUICK ROASTED CHICKEN

These days you can buy a precooked chicken from the supermarket—it's a great convenience item that I certainly rely upon from time to time. But the recipe here is all about the convenience of roasting your own chicken in minimal time; by removing the backbone of the chicken and roasting it flat, I can reduce the cooking time by a third. One of the beauties of roasting your own chicken, as opposed to buying a preroasted one, is that you know that yours is free of unnecessary additives and fat.

SERVES 4

1 (3½-pound) whole chicken
Olive oil
Salt and pepper to taste

1. Preheat the oven to 390°F (200°C).

2. Take chicken out of its packaging and pat it dry with a paper towel to remove any excess moisture. Then remove any giblets, the neck, or other extras that could be stuffed inside the cavity.

3. Place the chicken, breast side up, on a cutting board, and insert a large knife into the cavity of the chicken, cutting down along each side of the backbone, from the neck to the tail; remove the backbone. Place the chicken, breast side down, on the cutting board and use the heel of the knife to crack the breastbone of the chicken, allowing the chicken to flatten out even further.

4. Rub the chicken in olive oil and sprinkle with salt and pepper. Place it into a preheated ovenproof skillet to brown it, breast side down, until it turns golden, approximately 8–10 minutes, then turn it over. Place the skillet into the oven for approximately 25–30 minutes, or until the chicken is cooked through (the best way to check for doneness is to slip a knife between the thigh and rib cage to make sure any moisture that runs out is clear, not pink). Let the chicken rest on the stove top for another 10 minutes before carving and serving.

ROASTED BREAST OF CHICKEN STUFFED WITH FONTINA AND ROSEMARY

This dish is surprisingly simple to make and showcases the wonderful flavors of fontina cheese with rosemary, along with fingerling potatoes and baby spinach. Once you have mastered the art of stuffing a chicken breast, you will want to experiment with your own favorite taste sensations. If you don't eat cheese, for example, you can stuff the chicken breast with blanched and fresh herbs and greens like arugula, spinach, parsley, and sorrel. Besides adding a lovely surge of flavor, these green additions increase the moisture content in the chicken.

SERVES 2

2 cups small fingerling potatoes, rinsed and split in half lengthwise
6 whole cloves garlic
2 large sprigs rosemary
5 tablespoons olive oil, divided
Salt and freshly ground black pepper to taste
2 (6-ounce) chicken breasts, skin and wing bone intact
2 ounces fontina cheese
1 teaspoon finely chopped fresh rosemary
2 cups baby spinach
1 small lemon, cut into wedges

1. Preheat the oven to 375°F (190°C).

2. Place the potatoes onto a baking sheet with the garlic and rosemary, douse them with 3 tablespoons olive oil, and season with salt and pepper. Bake them for approximately 30 minutes or until they're golden and tender. Remove them from the oven and set them aside.

3. Meanwhile, hold the chicken breast by the wing and push your index finger between the flesh and the skin to separate the skin from the flesh and form a pocket. Repeat with the other breast.

4. Cut the cheese into 2 thin pieces, roll it in the chopped fresh rosemary, then push the cheese under the skin of the chicken breast.

5. Heat the remaining 2 tablespoons olive oil in an ovenproof frying pan. Season the chicken breasts with salt and pepper and, when the pan is hot, place the chicken into the pan, flesh side down, and brown it for 2 minutes. Turn it over and then place the pan into the oven for 8–10 minutes, which should be enough time for the chicken to cook through (however, a larger breast may take a bit longer to cook through).

6. Remove the pan from the oven, wrap the chicken in foil, and let it rest for 5 minutes before serving.

7. Toss the spinach with the hot potatoes, squeeze in a little lemon juice, and allow the spinach to wilt.

8. To serve, place a small bed of the potatoes, garlic, and spinach in the center of a plate. Use a sharp knife to slice the chicken into several pieces and lay it over the top of the potatoes. Serve with a lemon wedge.

CRISPY-SKIN SALMON WITH CAULIFLOWER, WHITE BEANS, AND ARUGULA

Here's a simple midweek meal that not only produces a tasty fish dish that's packed with omega-3 fatty acids, but also is gluten-free and super quick to get on the dining table. Keeping the skin on adds texture to the fish, and by roasting the fish skin side down in the pan, you will render out the fat and make the skin crisp. (If eating the skin doesn't appeal to you, simply remove and discard it before serving.)

SERVES 2

½ head small cauliflower, approximately 1 pound
3 tablespoons extra-virgin olive oil
1 clove garlic, peeled and finely chopped
⅓ cup water
1 (12-ounce) can white beans (cannellini), well drained
1 cup fresh arugula
Salt and freshly ground black pepper to taste
1 tablespoon olive or canola oil
2 (6-ounce) salmon fillets, bones removed and skin on
1 lemon, cut into wedges

1. Cut the cauliflower into small florets, peel the stalk, and cut it into bite-size pieces.

2. In a medium saucepan with a tight-fitting lid, heat the extra-virgin olive oil along with the chopped garlic for a few moments without letting it brown. Add the cauliflower and water, cover the pan with the lid, and allow the cauliflower to steam for 5 minutes; drain it and return it to the heat to brown a little. Add the white beans and continue cooking until all the ingredients are warmed through, then add the arugula leaves along with a pinch of salt and a good grinding of fresh pepper. Keep the veggies warm until you're ready to serve them.

3. Heat the olive or canola oil in a frying pan over a medium heat. Season the salmon with salt and pepper and place the fillets, skin side down, in the pan. Cook them for 3–4 minutes before turning them over and cooking for an additional 3–4 minutes on the other side; cooking time will vary depending on how thick the pieces of fish are.

4. To serve, place the salmon fillets alongside the cauliflower and white beans. Serve with a wedge of lemon.

SICILIAN CHICKPEA STEW

This is a meal that is full of flavor and texture, and the smell alone will transport you to Sicily! It's also relatively quick and simple to prepare, and it certainly won't break your budget. This stew, which I developed with Tahlia Gilbert, my second chef at the Bistro Moncur in Australia, where I was head chef, has become a staple in my personal kitchen, by itself or as a side dish.

SERVES 2

3 tablespoons olive oil

1 red onion, diced

1 large carrot, peeled and diced

1 celery stalk, peeled, leaves removed and diced

3 cloves garlic, peeled and left whole

1 teaspoon fennel seeds

½ teaspoon paprika

Juice and zest of 1 orange

½ cup dry white wine or verjuice*

1 (14-ounce) can chickpeas, drained

4 Roma tomatoes, peeled, seeded, and roughly chopped

6 large chard leaves, stalk removed and roughly shredded

3 tablespoons chopped flat-leaf parsley

Salt and freshly ground black pepper to taste

*Verjuice is an unfermented green grape juice that can be found in specialty food stores.

1. Heat olive oil in a large pan over medium heat and then add the onion, carrot, celery, garlic cloves, and fennel seeds. Cook the vegetables slowly for about 15 minutes, or until the carrots are tender. Add the paprika, orange zest and juice, and white wine or verjuice, and cook until the liquid is reduced by almost two-thirds.

2. Add the chickpeas, tomatoes, chard, and parsley. Finish with a good pinch of salt and pepper. Allow the dish to sit and steep away from the heat, covered, for 20 minutes before serving.

SLOW-ROASTED PORK SHOULDER WITH GARLIC, FENNEL, AND CHILI

This is another of those ideal recipes for feeding a large number of people on a budget; it's perfect as part of a Thanksgiving dinner or a large celebration. It definitely needs to spend a good length of time in the oven; you can't rush this process, and if you do, you will only end up with a tough pork shoulder. I recommend reading through the whole recipe before you start this one so you know what you're getting into; it's a good half-day process (though most of it doesn't require active involvement from you).

SERVES 12–15

1 (8- to 11-pound) pork shoulder, bone out and skin on
1 whole garlic bulb, peeled (roughly 10–12 cloves)
1½ tablespoons salt
3 heaping tablespoons fennel seeds
1 tablespoon dried chili flakes
¾ cup olive oil
2 cups chicken stock

1. Use a sharp knife to score the skin of the pork shoulder about ⅛ inch deep.

2. Use a mortar and pestle (or a food processor) to pound the garlic and salt to a rough purée; then add the fennel seeds and chili and continue to process. Once you have achieved a coarse paste, add the olive oil.

3. Rub the paste into the pork shoulder (both the flesh and the skin) and then roll the shoulder up and tie it with butcher's string at 2-inch intervals. Place the shoulder onto a wire rack and set it on a roasting pan. Leave it to sit unrefrigerated for a couple of hours (covered with a clean kitchen towel) to come to room temperature.

4. Preheat the oven to 460°F (240°C). Place the pork shoulder into the oven for 15 minutes, then drop the temperature to 220°F (105°C) and let it roast for 9 hours. To test if it's ready, push a skewer or a thin, sharp knife into the shoulder; when it's done, you should be able to push it in and pull it out with barely any resistance. Remove the pork shoulder from the oven and set it to rest over a cooling rack for a good hour, covered in foil.

5. Skim any excess fat off the baking sheet, reserving any pork roasting juices. Place the baking tray over direct medium heat on the stove and add the chicken stock; bring it to a boil and continue to simmer it for a good 8–10 minutes. Remove it from the heat and strain the liquid into a smaller saucepan. Check the seasoning to see if you want to add anything (you shouldn't need to, but everyone's palate is different). Set the liquid aside and keep warm until you're ready to serve.

6. Carve the shoulder minutes before you're ready to serve. Present it along with an assortment of side dishes, such as Honey-and-Thyme-Glazed Baby Carrots (see page 175), Roasted Beets (see page 181), and Parsley Purée (see page 200) and the reserved sauce.

THAI-STYLE SNAPPER
AND EGGPLANT CURRY

I love everything there is to love about Thai food—its simplicity in preparations and its complexity of flavors. The balance of sweet, sour, and salty varies from region to region, as does the use of chili. With this recipe, you'll want to adjust the flavoring to your liking—a little more lime juice here, a little more brown sugar there. . . . You get the idea!

SERVES 4

2 tablespoons vegetable oil

4 Japanese eggplants (the long, thin ones), split in half lengthwise

1 heaping tablespoon red curry paste

1 (12-ounce) can coconut cream

1-inch knob of ginger, peeled and finely sliced

2 tablespoons fish sauce

1 tablespoon brown sugar

Juice of 2 limes

1 pound snapper fillet or another firm white fleshed fish, boned and skinned

4 Thai eggplants (these look like golf balls), split in half (optional)

2 cups steamed rice

1 cup bean sprouts (see page 95)

2 tablespoons fried garlic chips (see page 84)

A handful of fresh basil leaves or Thai basil (if you can find it)

1. Heat a wok or a large saucepan with the vegetable oil, add the Japanese eggplants, flesh side down, and cook for a couple of minutes or until the eggplants are golden brown; turn them over and cook them for a couple more minutes. Remove them from the pan and set them aside.

2. In the same pan, drop in the curry paste along with one-third of the coconut cream and cook for a few minutes or until the cream "cracks" or splits and the curry paste becomes aromatic. Then add the ginger and the remaining coconut cream. Bring the mixture to a boil. Stir in the fish sauce, brown sugar, and lime juice.

3. Add the eggplant to the curry sauce and continue to cook over a low heat for 5–8 minutes, or until the eggplant is tender. Add the pieces of snapper and the Thai eggplant (if available); cover the wok or pan with a lid and allow the ingredients to steam for 2–3 minutes, or until the fish is cooked through.

4. Serve this dish immediately with steamed rice, topped with bean sprouts, crispy fried garlic, and basil.

STIR-FRIED RICE WITH ASPARAGUS AND OYSTER MUSHROOMS

In my house, the humble stir-fry is always welcome. A fast and efficient way to cook, this method lets you vary the ingredients, and it's a great way to use up leftovers. It's an easy way to get a delicious dinner on the table in a matter of minutes, using really fresh ingredients.

SERVES 1

1 tablespoon vegetable oil

1 clove garlic, peeled and thinly sliced

2 green onions (scallions), finely sliced on the diagonal, divided

½ teaspoon chili flakes

1 small handful oyster mushrooms

6 asparagus spears, tough ends discarded and finely sliced

¼ cup frozen peas

2 tablespoons water

1 cup cooked basmati or doongara rice

1 tablespoon tamari sauce

1 teaspoon sesame oil

1 fresh chili pepper, seeded and finely sliced

1. In a wok or a large saucepan, heat the vegetable oil along with the garlic over a medium heat. Once the garlic starts to take on a little color, add half the green onions along with the chili flakes and cook for 20–30 seconds before adding the mushrooms; once the mushrooms have wilted somewhat, add the asparagus, peas, and water, and sauté for a few moments.

2. Add the rice along with the tamari sauce and sesame oil; continue to heat the ingredients through by gently shaking and tossing the pan as you go.

3. Once the rice is hot, remove it from the heat and serve it with fresh chili slices and the reserved green onions.

WARM SALAD OF GRILLED SHRIMP, WHITE PEACH, AND ASPARAGUS

In the minds of my Australian and Kiwi families, a shrimp is a prawn. To all my American friends, you can't beat a big, fat king prawn—it's a bucket-list experience! In my opinion a king prawn's flavor and texture is superior to any shrimp I have had thus far. Whatever you choose to call these delicious little sea creatures, they are perfect in this warm weather salad that is loaded with flavor and intriguing textures. (Grilled scallops, lobster, or crab would also be delicious here.)
SERVES 2

1 bunch asparagus (approximately 12 spears), ends trimmed
1 firm but ripe peach
10 medium-size shrimp, peeled and deveined
Salt and freshly ground black pepper to taste
Fennel Vinaigrette (see page 198)
10 fresh basil leaves, torn

1. Blanch the asparagus in plenty of boiling salted water until the spears are tender, approximately 2–3 minutes; refresh them in cold water, drain well on paper towels, and cut them into 2-inch batons. Set aside.

2. Split the peach in half, remove the pit, and cut each half into quarters.

3. On a hot griddle pan, grill the shrimp, seasoned with salt and pepper, for several minutes on both sides until they're golden and cooked through.

4. While the prawns are still warm, toss them in the Fennel Vinaigrette, along with the asparagus, peach chunks, and torn basil. Serve at once.

chicken. Cook it for another 20 minutes or until the beans are tender. Mix the milk with the cornstarch and pour it into the pan. Continue cooking for another 10 minutes to thicken the sauce. Check the seasoning and adjust it, if necessary, with salt and pepper, adding additional cayenne pepper, if desired. Add the Monterey Jack cheese to the pot and stir to melt.

5. Serve the chili in a bowl. Garnish, as desired, with cilantro, sour cream, extra cheese—even pico de gallo and guacamole if you have some on hand. Roll up warmed corn tortillas and serve these on the side of the bowl.

CHAPTER SEVEN
ON THE SIDE

Whether they contain grains, legumes, or vegetables, side dishes can enhance just about any main dish and hence any meal. They bring variety to the table, adding complementary flavors and textures. Plus, they introduce other colors from Mother Nature's garden, which means an extra treat for your eyes and extra nutrients for your body!

There are many occasions when I'm cooking just for myself that I'll prepare three side dishes and call that dinner. (I have moments where my body just craves vegetables, so vegetable-based sides work well for me.) Side dishes are so versatile that you can incorporate them into lunch, dinner, and snacks. And if you keep sides in the healthy zone, you can help yourself cut back on your consumption of less healthful fare. Really, it's impossible to go wrong with good side dishes!

ASPARAGUS WITH CITRUS VINAIGRETTE

This great little side dish can accompany a piece of grilled fish, chicken, or pork. This is one of those recipes that illustrates just how quick and easy it can be to eat healthfully. If you can get your hands on white asparagus, try grilling it and serving it with the citrus vinaigrette, white peaches, and roasted scallops. Delish!

SERVES 4

1 bunch green asparagus, tough ends removed
1 ruby red grapefruit
1 orange
2 limes
⅓ cup olive oil
2 tablespoons red wine vinegar
1 teaspoon tamari sauce
1 teaspoon pink peppercorns
¼ bunch cilantro leaves, finely chopped
Salt and freshly ground black pepper to taste

1. Blanch the asparagus in plenty of boiling salted water until the stalks are tender, approximately 3 minutes. Remove from the boiling water and refresh the asparagus under cold running water; pat them dry with paper towels, and set them aside.

2. Remove the skin and pith from all the citrus fruits. Segment the fruit, separating the flesh using a small paring knife. Squeeze the remaining juice from the core of the citrus fruits into a bowl. Finely dice the segments and add them to the juice, along with the remaining ingredients.

3. Mix the ingredients gently to combine. If the salad tastes a little sharp, add more oil; if it's too oily, add a little more vinegar. Serve immediately.

BAKED SWEET POTATO FRIES

The key to a good baked sweet potato fry is to give the sweet potatoes plenty of space to cook. Don't overcrowd them or let them overlap while they're baking, because this will just cause them to become soggy. What we're looking for are crunchy, tasty fries! This recipe will help you get them just right. (By the way, these are delicious served with the lamb cutlets, as pictured on page 147.)

SERVES 4

4 medium sweet potatoes, scrubbed and dried
3 tablespoons olive oil
3 sprigs fresh rosemary, leaves stripped from the stalk
6 cloves garlic, bruised and left whole in the skin
Sea salt flakes and cracked black pepper, to taste

1. Preheat oven to 425°F (220°C).

2. Place each sweet potato on a cutting board and cut them into ¼-inch-thick slices lengthwise, then cut each slice into ¼-inch-thick fries.

3. Place the sweet potato sticks into a bowl and toss them with the olive oil, rosemary, garlic, sea salt flakes, and cracked black pepper.

4. Arrange them in a single layer on a baking sheet lined with parchment paper and bake them in the oven for approximately 35–40 minutes, until they turn golden and tender. Don't be tempted to shake them around too much while they're cooking; doing so will cause them to break up because of their high moisture content. But it won't hurt to flip them once to allow them to cook evenly.

5. After removing them from the oven, give them a few moments to cool before serving. Serve them by themselves or with a helping of fresh Aioli (see page 193).

BAKED BRUSSELS SPROUTS WITH DRIED FIGS, BACON, AND LEMON

I prefer to fry brussels sprouts, but since I want this book to be loaded with fun, delicious, and healthy recipes, I chose the baked route. They're very good this way, too! The bacon and figs add a rich flavor, with the contrasting elements of salty and sweet, and the lemon juice adds a pop of citrus. In fact, this is a great, well-rounded dish on its own.

SERVES 4

1 pound small brussels Sprouts
2 tablespoons olive oil
Salt and pepper to taste
2 tablespoons unsalted butter
8 slices of thick-cut bacon, finely chopped
½ cup dried figs, cut into small pieces
2 cloves garlic, peeled and chopped
1 lemon, cut into quarters
¼ cup chopped parsley

1. Preheat the oven to 425°F (220°C).

2. Peel away a few of the heavier dark leaves from the brussels sprouts, split them in half, and blanch them in a pot of boiling salted water until they're tender, approximately 4–5 minutes; remove them from the pot and refresh them in ice water for just a couple of minutes to stop the cooking process. Drain them well.

3. Toss the brussels sprouts in the olive oil with a little salt and pepper, then place them into a large ovenproof frying pan and pan roast them for a few moments over moderate to high heat. Add the butter and place the pan into the oven for about 25 minutes; the brussels sprouts should turn quite dark but they shouldn't burn.

4. Meanwhile, place the bacon in a smaller fry pan and set over a moderate heat; use a wooden spoon to give the bacon a stir every few moments to prevent it from sticking. Lower the heat and continue to cook the bacon for a few minutes, until it has dried out and the fat has separated. Remove the pan from the heat and pour off as much fat as possible; add the figs along with the garlic and cook them for a few moments, until the garlic takes on a little color.

5. Remove the brussels sprouts from the oven and add them to the bacon. Squeeze the juice from the lemon over the top, sprinkle with the parsley, and toss the ingredients gently. Adjust the seasoning, if necessary, and serve.

LITTLE RED POTATO SALAD

Here is a refreshing variation on potato salad, one that doesn't require a bucket of mayonnaise, which not only makes it egg-free but also vegan friendly. The onions and capers definitely give it a new flavor and feel. This will pair nicely with your next barbecued meal. Another variation on this dish is to replace the steamed potatoes with small chunks of roasted sweet potato.

SERVES 4

1 pound baby red potatoes, scrubbed clean
2 tablespoons extra-virgin olive oil
2 tablespoons balsamic vinegar
1 medium red onion, peeled and finely sliced
3 tablespoons baby capers (or chopped larger capers)
⅓ bunch flat-leaf parsley
Salt and freshly ground black pepper, to taste

1. Place the potatoes into a large pot of cold water, making sure they are all submerged, and set the pot over high heat. Bring the water to a boil, then reduce the heat to a simmer and continue to cook until the potatoes are tender, approximately 25–30 minutes. (The potatoes are cooked when a skewer or a small knife can be pushed into the potato without resistance.) Remove the pot from the heat, drain it, and set it aside.

2. Meanwhile, in a medium-size bowl, mix together the olive oil, balsamic vinegar, and onions. Add the hot potatoes and gently toss them; allow them to sit for 15 minutes while the onions soften before adding the capers and fresh parsley. Season with salt and pepper and serve.

ROASTED BEETS

There will always be room on my table for roasted beets: I love them for their vibrancy and earthy flavor. At any given time, I tend to roast twice as many as I need because they lend themselves to pretty much any meal, whether they're in a salad or a side dish. Roasting them individually, unpeeled, in foil helps maintain their vibrant earthy flavor as well as reducing the potential for beet-stained hands! If you'll be using larger beets, you can prepare them the same way; just cut them into smaller pieces before wrapping them in foil.

SERVES 4

1½ pounds red, gold, or other baby beets
2 tablespoons olive oil
Salt and freshly ground black pepper, to
   taste

1. Preheat the oven to 400°F (205°C).

2. Scrub the beets under cold running water to remove any dirt. Sprinkle them with olive oil and season them with salt and pepper.

3. Wrap each beet individually in foil and roast them in the oven for approximately 40 minutes. To test if they're ready, push a skewer into the largest of the beets; there should be no resistance. Once they're cooked through, remove the beets from the oven and let them cool in their foil for 20 minutes.

4. You can peel away the skin with your fingertips, but this isn't necessary if the beets have been scrubbed well.

SWISS CHARD WITH PINE NUTS AND CURRANTS

Swiss chard, rainbow chard, and spinach are all delicious served in this manner. This is a great accompaniment to roasted or grilled lamb or venison. The dried currants and garlic in this dish have a wonderful ability to mask the very earthy flavor that chard and spinach can sometimes offer. Even those who aren't fans of chard or spinach may become converts, thanks to this dish.
SERVES 4

1 large bunch swiss chard
3 cloves garlic, peeled and finely chopped
½ cup pine nuts
3 tablespoons olive oil
¼ cup currants
Salt and pepper, to taste
1 lemon, cut into quarters

1. Bring a large pot of water to boil and season it with salt.

2. Remove the stalks from the chard and place them into the pot of boiling salted water. Let them simmer for approximately 3–4 minutes, then remove them and refresh them in a bowl of ice-cold water (keeping the water boiling in the meantime). Once the stalks are cool, remove them from the water and set them to dry over paper towels. Finely slice them and set aside.

3. Place the chard leaves into the pot of boiling salted water and cook them for 2–3 minutes, or until they're tender. Remove them from the pot and refresh them in ice-cold water. Drain the leaves well and then chop them roughly.

4. In a large saucepan over moderate heat, sauté the garlic and pine nuts in the olive oil until they're golden. Add the chard leaves and stems along with the currants, and toss the ingredients gently to warm them through. Season the dish with salt and pepper and a good squeeze of lemon juice, and serve.

ZUCCHINI SPAGHETTI WITH BLACKENED TOMATOES

I will try just about anything to get kids more interested in eating vegetables. So far, my creative efforts have paid off personally: My ten-year-old son eats just about everything we put in front of him, including this delicious, nutrient-rich food. If this dish is a hit with your family, take note: The same method of taking thinly stripped zucchini and dousing it in olive oil and lemon juice can be applied to carrots, celery root, raw beets, shredded cabbage, and shaved raw artichokes.

SERVES 4

2 large green zucchini, approximately ¾ pound total (leave the skin intact)

Juice of 1 lemon

2 tablespoons extra-virgin olive oil

Salt and freshly ground black pepper, to taste

2 cups cherry tomatoes, one-third of them split in half

½ cup fresh mint leaves, larger leaves torn

1. To prepare the zucchini, use a large knife or a mandoline to remove the ends from the zucchini, then cut them into thin strips. (You may find it's easier to cut the zucchini into strips if you remove a thick slice from one side of the zucchini to give you a flat, stable surface to work on.) Then cut the zucchini strips into long straws by laying the slices flat on the board, a few at a time.

2. Place the zucchini, lemon juice, olive oil, and a little salt and pepper into a mixing bowl, lightly toss the ingredients, and then set them aside.

3. Place the tomatoes into a hot dry pan on top of the stove and roast on a high heat with a little salt and pepper until the tomatoes start to caramelize and the skins blacken. Remove the tomatoes from the heat, then toss with the raw zucchini and the torn mint leaves, and serve.

PAPER BAG MUSHROOMS

I love my mushies! When they're baked with a little additional seasoning (like in this recipe), they'll make your taste buds smile. This is such an easy side dish that it's suitable for pretty much any meal. Even though mushrooms aren't the most colorful of vegetables, it should be noted that they are low in calories, fat-free, cholesterol-free, and very low in sodium, yet they also provide important nutrients such as potassium, vitamin D, riboflavin, selenium, and more.

SERVES 2 AS A SIDE DISH

1 cup swiss brown mushrooms, baby bellas, or cremini mushrooms

1 cup oyster mushrooms

1 clove garlic, peeled and thinly sliced

3 sprigs fresh thyme (dried rosemary is another great option)

¼ teaspoon dried chili flakes (optional)

2 tablespoons olive oil

Juice of ¼ lemon

Salt and pepper, to taste

1. Preheat the oven to 400°F (205°C).

2. Cut the mushrooms into bite-size pieces (I generally slice them into quarters), place them into a medium-size bowl, and toss gently with the remaining ingredients.

3. Lay a piece of parchment paper about 12 inches long flat on the kitchen counter. Place the mushrooms on the center of the paper, take the edge of the parchment paper that's closest to you as well as the opposite edge, and bring them together above the mushrooms, folding the edges downward to create a tight pleat. Next, fold the left and right ends of the paper back under the mushrooms, creating a snug little parcel.

4. Place the parcel onto a heatproof tray, then put it into the preheated oven for approximately 10–12 minutes, or until the mushrooms are cooked.

ETCETERA: CONDIMENTS, SAUCES, AND DRESSINGS

AIOLI

This is pretty much a basic mayonnaise recipe (see page 195) with the addition of garlic. It's a great blank canvas for flavors that you like and appreciate (whether it's chopped chipotle, cilantro, or a little fresh horseradish). The aioli will stay perfectly fresh for up to a week in the refrigerator if it's stored in a sealed container.

MAKES ABOUT 1 CUP

3 cloves garlic
1 egg yolk
1 teaspoon smooth Dijon mustard
1 tablespoon lemon juice
Salt
1 cup olive oil
Freshly ground black pepper, to taste

1. Place the garlic into a small saucepan, cover with cold water, and place it over medium heat. Bring it to a boil, then strain the garlic, and repeat the process two more times. (This will remove the strong mustard characteristic of the garlic.) Allow the garlic to cool, then crush it.

2. In a bowl mix together the crushed garlic, egg yolk, mustard, lemon juice, and a good pinch of salt. Slowly and gradually pour in a fine stream of olive oil, whisking it simultaneously and continuously to create an emulsion of all the ingredients.

3. Fine-tune the seasonings and add a bit of freshly ground black pepper. If the mayonnaise tastes a little oily, add a touch more lemon juice. On the other hand, if it tastes a little too tart, then add a little more olive oil.

PARSLEY PURÉE

I love a good purée, especially to accompany a piece of roasted game meat, chicken, beef, or pork; the combination can be quite divine! You can play with different vegetables and herbs—everything from chard and pears to parsnips and apples to beets and horseradish—in this basic recipe. The key, though, is to make sure that whatever you're about to purée is cooked through and not too wet; a good purée should still have a little body to it. The seasonings are also important. The quantity you make will depend on the size of the bunch of herbs you use; with average-size bunches of parsley, this recipe should yield ½ to ¾ cup of purée.

1 clove garlic, peeled
1 large bunch curly-leaf parsley
1 large bunch flat-leaf parsley
2 tablespoons unsalted butter
Salt and ground white pepper, to taste
Ground nutmeg, to taste

1. Bring a medium pot of salted water to a boil with the garlic in it.

2. Plunge the parsley into a large bowl of cold water several times to release any dust and grit; drain it well then pat it dry with a towel. Pluck the leaves from each bunch of parsley, discarding the stalks. Drop the parsley leaves into the boiling water and cook for approximately 4–5 minutes, or until the parsley breaks down between your fingers but is still green. Quickly strain the parsley, discarding the clove of garlic and squeezing out most of the water (reserve a little so you can add it back to the purée).

3. While it's still hot, place the parsley into a blender and purée it. Add the butter, along with a small splash of the reserved parsley water, and purée until it's smooth.

4. Season the purée with a little salt, white pepper, and a hint of nutmeg, and serve.

CREAMY RICE PUDDING WITH ORANGE AND BUTTER-TOASTED ALMONDS

I love the texture and flavor of a sweet rice pudding. The addition of orange segments and almonds adds even more variety to the consistency and infuses the pudding with health-promoting nutrients. I once made this dish for five hundred people with my good friend and mentor Damien Pignolet: It was the dessert course for a special wine dinner in Sydney, and I will never forget the look on Damien's face when he saw me, literally up to my shoulders, folding whipped cream through the cooked rice in a very large commercial braising pan. To this day, making this dessert reminds me of the beauty of mentorship and that some things in life are worth a good laugh.

SERVES 4

3 oranges (2 to zest and segment and 1 to use for orange crisps*)

2 cups whole milk

1 vanilla bean, split in half lengthwise and scraped with the back of a knife to loosen the seeds (or 1 teaspoon vanilla extract)

½ cup Arborio rice

2 tablespoons unsalted butter

¼ cup blanched almonds, roughly chopped

¼ cup sugar

Pinch of salt

1 cup cream, whipped to semifirm peaks

*I find the easiest way to segment an orange is to remove the top and bottom of the orange using a serrated knife, stand it on a cutting board, and use a downward motion to follow the contour of the fruit to remove both skin and pith (the white part). Segment each orange fillet, separating the flesh with a small paring knife.

1. Preheat the oven to 210°F (100°C).

2. Thinly slice 1 orange (matchstick thin) with a sharp knife, then lay the slices out on a baking sheet lined with parchment paper. Place the baking sheet in the oven and leave it there for 1 hour. Remove and set these "orange crisps" aside. (These will stay fresh in an airtight container for several days.)

3. Bring the milk, the scraped vanilla bean, and the orange zest to a boil in a pot. Add the rice, lower the temperature, and cook, stirring it occasionally, for up to 20 minutes, or until the rice is tender.

4. In the meantime, heat the butter in a saucepan until it starts to foam; add the almonds and stir them with a wooden spoon until the nuts take on a lovely golden blush. Remove them from the heat and strain away the excess butter; set the almonds onto a paper towels to drain.

5. When the rice is tender and has absorbed all of the milk, mix in the sugar, along with a pinch of salt. Remove it from the saucepan and allow it to cool.

6. Just before serving, fold in the lightly whipped cream, the cooled almonds, and the fresh orange segments.

7. Serve the pudding in individual bowls and top with orange crisps.

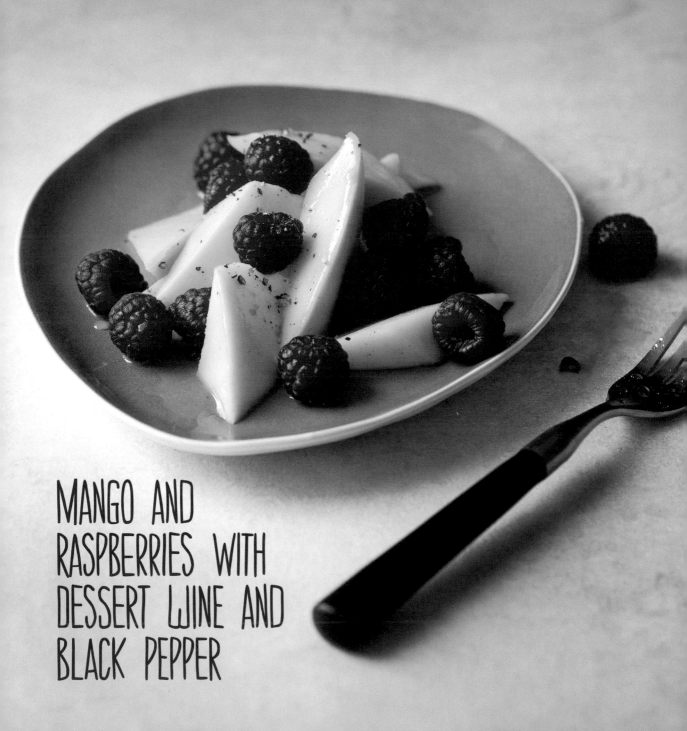

MANGO AND
RASPBERRIES WITH
DESSERT WINE AND
BLACK PEPPER

Here is a dessert that is nothing short of delicious and absolutely convenient when you're short on time. Alternatively, you can prepare fresh figs, peaches, apricots, or strawberries the same way. What makes this dessert so decadent is the balance of sweet and spicy! The pepper and dessert wine are a wonderful combination that I really insist you try.

SERVES 2

2 ripe mangoes
½ cup dessert wine
1 cup fresh raspberries
A few mint leaves (optional)
Cracked black pepper
¼ cup crème fraîche or sour cream

1. Cut the cheeks (the flesh from each side of the pit) from each side of the mangoes. Remove the skin and cut the flesh into large chunks. Place them in a bowl, douse them in dessert wine, and cover and chill them in the fridge for 20 minutes.

2. Gently fold in the raspberries and optional torn mint leaves.

3. Before serving, sprinkle the fruit with a little fresh cracked black pepper. Serve on a small plate or in a martini-style glass, drizzled with a little crème fraîche or sour cream. Bon appétit!

DARK CHOCOLATE AND TOASTED WALNUT BROWNIE BITES WITH SALTED CARAMEL

This is a gluten-free version of the Bittersweet Chocolate and Toasted Walnut Brownie that I used to serve at the Bellevue Hotel in Sydney. There was always a mad frenzy for the offcuts (the scraps) when they were being portioned out—they were that good! Even the gluten-free version is my personal must-have sweet treat. Once you try it, you will understand why! This recipe will make about eighty 1-inch squares; I like to freeze half of the cooled brownies then defrost them half an hour before I'm ready to serve them.

APPROXIMATELY 80 (1-INCH) SQUARES

1⅓ cups bittersweet dark chocolate buttons or chocolate chips
13 tablespoons plus 1 teaspoon unsalted butter (or ⅞ cup)
1 vanilla bean, split and scraped (or 1 teaspoon vanilla extract)
3 large eggs
1 cup sugar
1½ cups almond meal or ground almond flour
1½ cups toasted, chopped walnuts
Freshly whipped cream, for serving

1. Preheat the oven to 350°F (175°C).

2. Line a 9-inch square baking pan with parchment paper and set it aside.

3. Place the chocolate, butter, and vanilla bean into a medium-size bowl and set it over a saucepan of gently simmering water (make sure the bowl does not come into direct contact with the water). Once the chocolate has melted, remove the bowl from the heat and allow the chocolate to cool for 5 minutes. After this, you can discard the vanilla bean.

4. Meanwhile, beat the eggs and sugar in a separate bowl until they're light and fluffy. Fold them into the chocolate mixture, along with the almond meal or almond flour and toasted, chopped walnuts.

5. Pour the chocolate-and-nut batter into the prepared cake pan and bake in the preheated oven for 25–30 minutes, or until the top looks slightly crusty but the center is still a little soft when pierced with a skewer. Remove the pan from the oven and allow it to cool for 10–15 minutes before turning the brownies out onto a cake rack.

6. Once the brownie has cooled and is somewhat firm, cut it up into 1-inch squares. Serve with a little helping of Salted Caramel Sauce (recipe follows) and freshly whipped cream.

Salted Caramel Sauce

Resist the temptation to stick your finger into the sweet goo while you're making it because it is molten hot! I have been burned several times doing this; also, be mindful of the steam that's created when you add the cream and butter.

MAKES 1½ CUPS

1 cup sugar
½ cup water
½ cup heavy cream
2 tablespoons unsalted butter
½ teaspoon sea salt flakes

1. Place the sugar and water into a heavy-bottomed pan and set it over moderate heat on the stove. Stir the mixture until the sugar has dissolved.

2. Increase the heat and boil the mixture until the sugar starts turning amber in color, approximately 6–8 minutes. At this point, watch the pan closely because the mixture can go dark quickly: As soon as it reaches a slightly deeper amber color, remove the pan from the heat.

3. Carefully whisk in the cream followed by the butter. Once it is well mixed, put it in a fresh bowl to cool. Sprinkle with the sea salt flakes when you serve the sauce.

BUTTERMILK PUDDING

This pudding is not unlike a panna cotta in texture, but I think the flavor is superior. It holds a lot more character due to the buttermilk's tartness. This particular dish is reminiscent of my time as a pastry chef at Bistro Moncur, and it's one of the many desserts I personally adore.

MAKES 6 (½-CUP) SERVINGS

3 teaspoons powdered gelatin
2 tablespoons warm water
⅓ cup cream
¾ cup sugar
½ vanilla bean, seeds removed and reserved
2⅓ cups buttermilk
½ cup heavy cream, whipped to stiff peaks
2 small baskets raspberries
2 tablespoons confectioners' sugar
1 lime

1. Soak the powdered gelatin in warm water.

2. Heat the cream, sugar, and vanilla seeds together in a small saucepan over medium heat until the sugar has dissolved. Stir in the dissolved gelatin. Allow the mixture to cool, stirring from time to time.

3. Stir in the buttermilk, then fold the whipped cream into the buttermilk base and fill the individual molds or ramekins. Chill for at least 4 hours before serving.

4. Purée half the raspberries with the confectioners' sugar and a squeeze of lime juice until the mixture is smooth.

5. To serve the pudding, dip the molds into hot water, then use a small knife to release the cream by tilting the mold and gently sliding the knife down the side of the cream. Invert the pudding onto a plate, and serve with the puréed raspberries and the remaining fresh raspberries.

DARK CHOCOLATE TRUFFLES

There's just no way around it: These truffles are a little slice of heaven! The best thing to do is make a batch, eat two, and then give the rest away. Good luck with that! But if you can swing it, you'll make a lot of people in your world very happy.

MAKES APPROXIMATELY 30 WALNUT-SIZE TRUFFLES

1 vanilla bean (or 1 teaspoon vanilla extract) (optional)
⅔ cup heavy cream
⅓ cup sugar
1⅓ cups bittersweet dark chocolate, chopped into small pieces
2 tablespoons unsalted butter
¾ cup dark unsweetened cocoa
Sea salt flakes

1. If using, split the vanilla bean in half lengthwise with a small knife, then run the back of the knife along the inside of both halves to release the tiny seeds.

2. In a medium saucepan over a moderate heat, bring to a boil the cream, sugar, and vanilla bean. Once it boils, pour in the chocolate and butter, and mix well until the chocolate has melted and is smooth in texture.

3. Leave the vanilla bean in the chocolate and let the mixture stand at room temperature for 20 minutes before placing it in the refrigerator to set.

4. Once the mixture has set and turned quite firm, remove the vanilla bean, place the mixture into a piping bag, and pipe it into little teardrops on a chilled tray that's been lined with aluminum foil or parchment paper. (I find that a size 8 plain nozzle works best for piping the chocolate.) Alternatively, take a warm (but not wet) teaspoon and pull it through the chocolate to give you small pieces. Chill the pieces for another hour.

5. Remove the chocolate from the refrigerator and, with clean hands, roll it into balls. Drop each truffle into the cocoa and toss it until it's completely coated. Keep the truffles refrigerated until 10 minutes before serving, then sprinkle sea salt flakes on top and present these beauties.

BOILED ORANGE AND
ALMOND CAKE

I first saw this cake being made during my time as an apprentice at Ravesis in Bondi, Australia—and I was amazed at the idea of boiling oranges for 2 hours until they were soft! This cake and its ingredients have no resemblance to the cakes my mum or nana made (apart from the eggs and sugar). Over the years, this has become one of my favorite cakes for its simplicity, flavor, texture, and freedom from gluten. Surprisingly, I find this cake gets better with age because it starts drying out around the edges and gets a nice chewy-marzipan sort of texture.

SERVES 12: 1 (10-INCH) CAKE PAN OR 3 (6 X 3½-INCH) LOAF PANS

2 large oranges (organic, if possible)
1 tablespoon unsalted butter
1½ tablespoons plus 1 cup sugar, divided
5 eggs
2⅓ cups ground almond flour/almond meal
1 teaspoon baking powder
Pinch of salt
Confectioners' sugar
Freshly whipped cream

1. Place the oranges in a saucepan and cover them with cold water. Take a piece of parchment paper and set it over the oranges, then put a plate (or a suitable weight) on top to keep the oranges from floating upward. Bring the water to a rolling boil, lower the heat, and simmer for 2 hours. Remove the pan from the heat and allow the oranges to cool.

2. Once the oranges have cooled, split them into quarters, leaving the skin intact. Remove as many seeds as possible and roughly chop the oranges.

3. Preheat the oven to 375°F (190°C).

4. Butter a baking pan evenly with 1 tablespoon butter and then dust it with 1½ tablespoons sugar to create a nonstick coating.

5. Place the oranges, including skin, and the eggs into a food processor or blender and purée until the mixture is smooth.

6. In a separate bowl, mix the ground almonds, 1 cup sugar, and baking powder. Whisk the orange and egg mixture into the almond mixture until it's well incorporated.

7. Pour the batter into the prepared cake pan, place it into the oven, and bake for approximately 70 minutes. The cooking time may vary as the cake being quite dense in texture; I find the best way to test for doneness is to push a skewer in—it should be relatively cake-free when you pull it out.

8. Allow the cake to cool, then dust it with confectioners' sugar and top it with a little freshly whipped cream before serving.

BAKED STUFFED PEACHES

This recipe is a little play on a classic crumble dessert. I used to serve this at Bistro Moncur in Sydney with fresh cream that was whipped with some sugar and Amaretto. This is a "Can I please have more?" sort of dish. By baking the naturally sweet peaches, you reduce their moisture content and increase their flavor profile even more, making them absolutely incredible.

SERVES 4

4 large ripe peaches (they should be firm but
    not hard, soft but not mushy)
¼ cup crushed amaretti biscuits (Italian
    almond-flavored macaroons; I use gluten-
    free amaretti)
¼ cup almond meal or ground almond flour
2 tablespoons brown sugar
2 tablespoons unsalted melted butter
Juice of 1 lemon
3–4 tablespoons water
1 tablespoon granulated sugar
Freshly whipped cream

1. Preheat the oven to 375°F (190°C).

2. Immerse the peaches in boiling water for 10–20 seconds, then plunge them into ice-cold water. Carefully peel away the skins, cut them in half, and remove the stones.

3. Scoop out about a teaspoon of flesh from each of the peaches and place it into a mixing bowl with the crushed amaretti, almond meal or almond flour, brown sugar, butter, and a little lemon juice to help moisten the mixture.

4. Pile the stuffing into each peach half, place the halves onto a shallow ovenproof tray surrounded by the water (the water helps steam the peaches), and sprinkle the peaches with the granulated sugar.

5. Bake the stuffed peaches for 25–30 minutes, or until their toppings are golden. The peaches should still hold their shape but should be tender when pierced with a skewer or small knife.

6. Serve the peaches with a small dollop of freshly whipped cream.

FRESH STRAWBERRIES WITH GIANNI'S ZABAGLIONE

Zabaglione is a creamy mousse-like, melt-in-your-mouth dessert topping. Not only is it simple to make but it's also a super luscious way to finish any meal. The recipe below is from a good friend of mine, Gianni Mancuso, who happens to be one of the most eccentric untrained cooks I know. If you're not in the mood for strawberries, feel free to work with different fruits—stone fruits (peaches, nectarines, and apricots) work amazingly, as will most berries.

SERVES 2

2 cups fresh strawberries
½ cup Marsala wine, divided (Marsala is a
   sweet, dark wine from Italy. If you can't
   find it, you could use the same amount of
   a good Muscat or Amaretto.)
4 tablespoons sugar
4 egg yolks

1. Wash and pick through the berries, discarding any bruised or rotten ones. Pour half the Marsala over the berries, and allow them to sit for a few moments at room temperature.

2. Meanwhile, bring a medium-size saucepan of water to a simmer. Place a stainless steel or glass bowl above the steaming pot of water; do not let the bowl touch the water.

3. Add the sugar, yolks, and other half of the Marsala to the bowl and beat it with a whisk or electric beater until it has tripled in volume, approximately 10–12 minutes. (The trick here is to beat it consistently, no matter how tired your arm gets; the goal is to beat air into it.) Once it has tripled in volume, remove it from the heat and set it aside. On its own, the volume will start to decrease, and the mixture will thicken.

4. Split the berries between two serving bowls, place the zabaglione over the top while it's still warm, and serve immediately.

EVE'S CHOCOLATE CAKE

Eve's Chocolate Cake is one of the classic dessert dishes that never left the Bistro Moncur menu during my seven years there. It's a tried-and-true flourless chocolate cake that came from my good friend and mentor Damien Pignolet. (The name Eve refers to a friend and colleague of Damien's.) This is a very rich cake, one that's usually reserved for special occasions. The better the chocolate you buy, the better the cake will be; if you can afford it, I highly recommend Valrhona chocolate. The trick with this recipe is that most things have to be ready at once.

SERVES 10

12 large eggs, separated (be careful not to
   get yolks in your whites)
1.8 ounces (50 grams) plus 2.1 ounces (60
   grams) granulated sugar
12 ounces (340 grams) bittersweet dark
   chocolate
3.5 ounces (100 grams) unsalted butter
Pinch of salt
¼ teaspoon cream of tartar
1⅓ cups heavy cream
¼ cup dark cocoa powder

1. Grease and line a 10-inch springform cake pan with parchment paper. Preheat the oven to 320°F (160°C).

2. With an electric mixer, beat the 12 egg yolks with 1.8 ounces (50 grams) sugar until it's almost white, approximately 5 minutes; the mixture should look creamy and velvety when it's finished.

3. In a separate bowl that's set over a pot of steaming (not boiling) water, melt the chocolate with the butter, stirring until the butter and chocolate are combined and the mixture is free of lumps.

4. In another large bowl, beat the 12 egg whites with a pinch of salt and cream of tartar until they have doubled in volume. At this point, gradually add 2.1 ounces (60 grams) sugar, a little at a time, while beating the egg whites until semifirm peaks form.

5. Mix the beaten yolks into the melted chocolate. Fold the egg whites, a third at a time, through the chocolate mixture, being careful not to knock all the air out of the whites while you're combining the ingredients.

6. Place two-thirds of the mixture into the prepared cake pan. Bake for 40 minutes in the preheated oven, or until a skewer pushed into the center comes out clean. Remove the cake from the oven, and invert it onto a cake rack to cool; you'll notice the cake will sink in the middle to create a well of sorts—don't worry: this is normal.

7. While the cake bakes, place the remaining chocolate mixture on the bottom shelf of your fridge to cool for approximately 1 hour.

8. Whip the cream until it forms semifirm peaks, then fold it into the chilled chocolate mousse. Place the new mixture back into the refrigerator until the cake has cooled completely. Once that has happened, fill the top of the cake with the mousse, dust the cake with cocoa powder, and set it aside until you're ready to serve it. (If you have leftover chocolate mousse, put it in individual cups and serve it with fresh berries and cream at a later date.)

Note: A hot, dry knife is best for cutting this cake.

FRESH FRUIT STICKS WITH LIME AND CHILI SYRUP

Here's a real feel-good dessert: It requires minimal effort, it's low in fat, and it's so refreshing. There is no set type of fruit to use; however, it should reflect the season and what's available and especially good at the time! I like to make the fruit look nice and uniform (save the offcuts for fresh juice or a smoothie the next day).

MAKES 6

¼ cup sugar

¼ cup water

½ small red chili, seeds removed, finely chopped (or ¼ teaspoon chili flakes)

Juice and zest of 1 lime

2 mangoes, ripe yet firm

1 small papaya, watermelon, or cantaloupe

1 basket strawberries, hulled

½ small pineapple

2 kiwi fruit, peeled and cut into bite-size chunks

Bamboo skewers to thread the fruit

1. Bring the sugar, water, chili, and lime juice and zest to a boil in a pot. Simmer for 2 minutes, then remove it from the heat and allow it to cool.

2. Cut the cheeks (the flesh from either side of the pit) from each of the mangoes. Remove the skin and cut each cheek in half. Then, cut each piece of mango into three mouthful-size pieces.

3. Split the papaya, watermelon, or cantaloupe in half, peel away the skin, and discard the seeds. Cut the skin off of the pineapple. Cut the papaya and the pineapple into similar mouthful-size pieces.

4. Thread the fruit onto skewers.

5. To serve, brush each skewer with the lime and chili syrup. Enjoy!

HAZELNUT CRÈME
CARAMEL

This is not a quick dessert to prepare, but it certainly ranks up there when it comes to deliciousness. It's best to read through the recipe a couple of times before tackling it, just so you're aware of each stage. Making a basic baked cream custard is a challenge for most people; be patient, you can't rush or force this but it is *so* worth the time and effort. (*Note:* You can reserve the additional whites for making meringues or omelets; they will keep perfectly well frozen.)

SERVES 4

1¾ cups shelled hazelnuts
1 cup milk
1¾ cups cream
1⅓ cups sugar, divided
4 tablespoons water, divided
2 whole eggs
4 egg yolks
Juice of 1 lime (optional)
4 tablespoons hazelnut liqueur (optional,
    Frangelico preferred)

1. Preheat the oven to 345°F (175°C).

2. Place the hazelnuts on a small baking sheet and roast in the oven until they're brown and you can begin to smell their roasting aroma, approximately 10–12 minutes.

3. Chop the hazelnuts roughly and place them into a small saucepan along with the milk and cream. Heat until the liquid is almost boiling, remove the pan from the heat, and allow it to sit for 30 minutes so the milk and cream can take on the hazelnut flavor.

4. Reduce the oven temperature to 285°F (140°C).

5. For the caramel, place ⅓ cup sugar in another small pan along with 2 tablespoons water, and stir over a low heat until the

water has been absorbed by the sugar. Bring the mixture to a boil and cook for another 6–7 minutes, or until the syrup has turned an amber color, then quickly add 2 more tablespoons water to stop the cooking process. While the syrup is still hot, distribute it evenly into four ⅔-cup molds (I use coffee cups)—be careful as the caramel is very hot! Pick up each mold, tilt it to the side and run the caramel around the inside of the mold, trying to coat as much of the base and walls of the mold as possible.

6. In a bowl gently beat the eggs and egg yolks along with the remaining 1 cup sugar until the mixture is creamy in color; gradually pour in the hazelnut milk, including the nuts, and use a spoon to mix it for a few moments (do your best not to aerate the mixture, since this will only cause bubbles in your custard).

7. Once it's well mixed, strain the contents of the bowl into a pouring jug, and discard the hazelnuts.

8. Pour the hazelnut cream into the six caramel-lined molds, and skim off any bubbles.

9. Place the molds into a deep-sided baking pan; add enough simmering water to the pan to come halfway up the outsides of the molds.

10. Cover the pan with foil, then place the pan (with the molds on it) into the oven and bake for 45–55 minutes. They will be ready when there is a slight wobble to the center of the caramel when the pan is shaken, but it should definitely not be runny.

11. Remove the pan from the oven and allow to stand at room temperature for 20 minutes, then chill all the molds in the refrigerator for a couple of hours before serving.

12. To serve, run a small knife around the edge of each mold, tilting the mold to the side to release the suction, and then turn the crème caramel out onto a small plate. Sprinkle with a little fresh lime juice and Frangelico, if desired.

LOADED CARAMEL POPCORN

Whether served as a dessert or as a snack, loaded caramel popcorn is one of my favorites. If you're making it in advance, be sure to store it in an airtight container once it's cool.
MAKES 6 (1-CUP) SERVINGS

1 cup brown sugar
½ cup unsalted butter
½ cup honey
½ teaspoon salt
½ teaspoon vanilla extract
½ teaspoon baking soda
4 cups freshly popped corn
¾ cup chopped toasted almonds or peanuts (optional)

1. Preheat the oven to 270°F (135°C).

2. In a large saucepan mix the sugar, butter, honey, and salt. Stir over medium heat until it boils. Continue to boil the mixture for 2–3 minutes, stirring occasionally. Remove the pan from the heat and add the vanilla and baking soda. Pour in the popcorn and nuts (if using). Mix well to coat evenly and place the pan into the oven and bake it for about 30 minutes, stirring occasionally.

3. Remove the pan from the oven and pour the mixture out onto a tray covered with parchment paper; once it has cooled, break it apart and store it in an airtight, covered container.

JACQUES APPLE

I had the good fortune of working alongside Jacques and Claudine Pépin at the fabulous food show in Cleveland, Ohio, in November 2012. Watching them cook together, I was inspired; in fact, like a kid in a candy store, I was mesmerized. The sight reinforced my love for being in the kitchen with my own family.

That day, Jacques cooked several dishes. But the one that stood out for me was his baked apple, not just because it was a dessert, but because here was a man of the kitchen, with so many years of experience, and while he could cook whatever he wanted, he chose to work with a simple, humble apple. The result was nothing short of incredible! This is his recipe (which you can find on page 472 of his cookbook *Essential Pépin* for Good Lady Apples—aka Apples Bonne Femme). On the day Jacques appeared onstage he made a last-minute addition to his apples by adding pecans and dates to form a stuffing. The recipe below incorporates this new and very welcome addition.

SERVES 6

6 large apples (choose a type that will keep its shape while it's cooking—Golden or Red Delicious, Russet, Granny Smith, or Pippin)

¼ teaspoon ground cinnamon or nutmeg, plus extra for dusting the apples

1 cup roughly chopped pecans

1 cup roughly chopped pitted dates

4 tablespoons cold unsalted butter, cut into tiny pieces, divided

⅓ cup apricot jam

⅓ cup maple syrup

1 cup sour cream

1. Preheat the oven to 375°F (190°C).

2. Core the apples using a corer or small knife. Be sure to plunge the corer or knife straight down so that it doesn't miss the core; if this happens, remove any remaining seeds.

3. Mix the cinnamon or nutmeg, pecans, dates, and half the butter in a small bowl, then set aside.

4. With the point of the knife, make an incision one-third of the way down each apple and cut through the skin, ⅛–¼ inch deep, all the way around. As the apple cooks the flesh will expand, and the part of the apple above this cut will lift up like a lid. Arrange the apples in a gratin dish large enough to accommodate all the apples and attractive enough to be brought to the table. Gently fill the empty center of each apple with the spice-nut-date mixture.

5. Coat the apples with the apricot jam and maple syrup, dot with remaining butter and a little extra sprinkle of cinnamon or nutmeg (if using), and bake for 30 minutes. Baste the apples with the juice and cook them for another 30 minutes; the apples should be cooked throughout and be plump, golden brown, and soft to the touch.

6. The apples look best when they have just emerged from the oven, puffed from the heat and glossy with a rich color. But it's best to serve them barely lukewarm and with a little sour cream.

LAVENDER MARSHMALLOWS

I couldn't resist including a recipe for my marshmallows. They are totally messy to make and a little time consuming, but they are such a treat, and people are always impressed when you tell them you made these yourself. The best part (for me) is that they are gluten-free, and they will keep in an airtight container for up to a week, providing you don't overindulge! Every now and then, I will dust the marshmallow using toasted coconut instead of cornstarch. There are some tools you will need for this recipe: a candy thermometer and a mixer with a whisk attachment.

MAKES ABOUT 70 (1-INCH) CUBES

1 tablespoon vegetable oil (or olive oil spray)

¼ cup plus ½–1 cup cornstarch

2 cups sugar

1 vanilla bean, split in half and scraped or ½ teaspoon vanilla extract (optional)

½ cup light corn syrup

⅓ cup chemical-free lavender flowers

2½ cups water, at room temperature, divided

¼ teaspoon salt

3½ (¾-ounce) packets unflavored gelatin

3 egg whites

¼ level teaspoon cream of tartar

Pinch of salt

1. Brush or spray the base and insides of a 9 x 13-inch rectangular pan with a little of the oil, then dust it with ¼ cup cornstarch to coat it evenly. Tap the pan on the sides to remove any excess cornstarch; reserve this for the top.

2. In a medium-size saucepan, combine the sugar, vanilla bean seeds, corn syrup, lavender, 1½ cups water, and the salt, and set the pan over a medium to low heat, stirring frequently until the sugar has dissolved. Increase the heat and bring the mixture to a boil, then continue to boil it until it reaches the soft-ball stage, or a temperature of 240°F (115°C) using a candy thermometer; this takes a good 12–15 minutes.

3. Meanwhile, place 1 cup water along with the gelatin in the base of the mixer and set it to a low speed.

4. When the syrup has reached the soft-ball stage (240°F [115°C]), remove the candy thermometer from the saucepan and pour the sugar syrup slowly into the mixer while it runs at low to medium speed. Once all the syrup has been added, increase the mixer speed to high and run it for another 7–8 minutes, or until the mixture has tripled in volume and cooled.

5. In a separate (clean) bowl, use a whisk to beat the egg whites with the cream of tartar and the salt until they have tripled in volume and stiff peaks have formed. Fold the whites into the beaten sugar mixture until evenly incorporated.

6. Pour and scrape this mixture into the prepared cake pan, sift the remaining cornstarch over the top of the marshmallow, and set the pan, uncovered, aside for 4–5 hours in a cool room to set.

7. Once the marshmallow has set, carefully remove it from the cake pan onto a clean and dry cutting board. Use a large, oiled knife and cut it into 1- to 1½-inch cubes; place the cubes onto a large tray that's been scattered with the additional cornstarch. Roll each marshmallow in the cornstarch to coat all sides; shake off the excess starch and pack the marshmallows into an airtight container until you're ready to serve them.

POACHED PEAR WITH STRAWBERRY COULIS AND VANILLA ICE CREAM

When done right, a poached pear can make for a stunning dessert. You can take it to another level by smothering it with a rich bittersweet chocolate sauce, or serve it with fresh vanilla ice cream—either way it's just divine. This is a recipe I knocked out one Sunday, while I was home alone. (For those who are vegan, simply replace the ice cream with coconut cream.)

SERVES 4

4 cups cold water
1½ cups sugar
Juice and zest of 1 lemon
1 vanilla bean, split lengthwise, seeds
    scraped and reserved (optional)
4 medium-size pears (Beurre, Bosc, or
    William, if possible)
1½ cups strawberries, hulled
½ cup confectioners' sugar
1 lime
4 scoops vanilla ice cream

1. In a pot that's large enough to hold the first five ingredients, place the water, sugar, lemon juice and zest, and vanilla bean plus the seeds. Stir the ingredients until the sugar has almost dissolved before you turn on the heat. Peel the pears and, leaving them whole, place them into the liquid.

2. Cover the pot with a piece of parchment paper to eliminate any moisture loss. Place the pot over medium heat and bring it to a boil.

3. Once the pears have reached the boiling point, remove the pot from the heat and allow the pears to cool in the same pot. Do not refrigerate them, as this could affect their sensuous texture. Once the pears have cooled to room temperature, you may refrigerate them for later use.

4. To make the strawberry coulis, place the strawberries and confectioners' sugar into a food processor and purée until they're a smooth consistency. Scrape the contents of the food processor into a fine-mesh sieve and use a spatula to work the strawberry coulis through the sieve, discarding the seeds. Squeeze in a little lime juice to mask the sweetness and lend balance to the flavor.

5. To serve, drain the pears well, and slice a little piece from the base of each pear to help it stand up. Place each pear into a bowl along with a scoop of ice cream, spoon the strawberry coulis over the pear, and serve!

Note: The pear poaching syrup can be used to poach more fruit or to sweeten cocktails.

RASPBERRY SOUFFLÉ

This is one of those impressive desserts that has a high *wow!* factor. Soufflés were once a dreaded dessert among cooks, because many people experienced a high rate of disaster with them. Once you master this recipe, feel free to stake your claim as soufflé king or queen; I certainly have. I love making this because it's gluten- and fat-free—at least until I add a spoonful of freshly whipped cream to it. You can prepare these up to 6 hours in advance.

MAKES 8 (1-CUP) SOUFFLÉ MOLDS

Butter to grease the dishes

Sugar to dust the interior of the dishes

1½ cups raspberry purée (approximately 2 small baskets of raspberries puréed)

1 cup sugar, divided

3 level tablespoons cornstarch

10.1 fluid ounces (300 ml) egg whites (approximately 10), free of any yolk

Pinch of cream of tartar

Confectioners' sugar, for dusting

Fresh whipped cream (optional)

1. Preheat the oven to 380°F (195°C).

2. Prepare each soufflé mold by lightly brushing the interiors with a thin layer of butter, adding the sugar, and coating evenly; discard any loose sugar. Set aside.

3. In a small saucepan, place two-thirds of the raspberry purée along with ½ cup sugar and set over a medium heat. Mix the remaining raspberry purée and the cornstarch with a wooden spoon, then add this to the heating purée and beat it with a whisk until it has thickened; continue to cook it for another 8–10 minutes over a low heat.

4. Place the mixture into a sieve and work it through, removing the seed content. Set it aside to cool.

5. Beat the egg whites to semifirm peaks, either by hand or with an electric mixer on medium speed. (Personally, I find the electric mixer very helpful.) While you're beating the egg whites, add the cream of tartar and continue to mix until it's well incorporated and fluffy (approximately 1 minute). Then increase the speed and slowly start to add the remaining ½ cup sugar, a little at a time. The egg whites should almost triple in volume and hold semifirm peaks.

6. Start incorporating the egg white mixture into the raspberry fruit base; this will need to be done in thirds. The first addition can be quite liberal but needs to be mixed well; the second addition of whites needs to be a little gentler, and the last third even gentler.

7. Fill each prepared mold to the top, leveling the mixture with a spatula and tapping the molds gently to remove any air bubbles. Run your thumb around the outside rim of the top of each soufflé mold to create a clear track for the soufflé to rise evenly.

8. At this point you can bake the soufflés or set them aside in the refrigerator (up to 6 hours) until you're ready to bake and serve them. Place the soufflés into the preheated 380°F oven and cook until they've risen by at least a third, approximately 8–10 minutes. Remove the soufflés from the oven, dust them with confectioners' sugar, and serve them with fresh whipped cream, if desired.

A VERY RICH
DOUBLE CHOCOLATE
MOUSSE WITH WALNUT
PRALINE AND FRESH CREAM

What's not to love about a good chocolate mousse? This is a delicious, sexy dish to prepare ahead of time, and it's portion controlled to boot. It is a favorite recipe from my time as head chef at the Bellevue Hotel in Sydney. I love working with the Valrhona bittersweet chocolate; I am a big believer that the better the chocolate is, the better the product will turn out to be. I have made it a little more decadent by pouring a thin layer of dark chocolate on top, to give the mousse a little more texture and character. The best way to really appreciate this little pot of heaven is to get a little bit of everything on your spoon or fork.

SERVES 8

For the Walnut Praline
1 cup walnut pieces
½ cup sugar
3 tablespoons water

For the Mousse
2⅓ cups plus ½ cup chopped dark chocolate
2 cups heavy cream
4 eggs
¼ cup triple sec (Cointreau preferred)
½ cup additional dark chocolate, melted in a
    clean dry bowl over steaming water
Fresh whipped cream, for serving
Sea salt flakes

1. Preheat the oven to 345°F (175°C).

2. Place the walnuts on a baking sheet and set them in the oven for approximately 10–12 minutes, or until they're golden. Remove them from the oven and set aside.

3. Meanwhile, combine the sugar and water in a saucepan over low heat until the sugar has dissolved thoroughly. Increase the heat and cook until the sugar takes on an amber, caramelized color. (Don't walk away from the sugar while it's cooking because it can burn quickly; if it burns or smells burned, you'll have to start again.) Remove the sugar mixture from the heat and quickly mix the nuts into it, using a swirling action, then turn the new mixture out onto a clean baking sheet. Spread the nuts and sugar level with a spatula. Let it cool to room temperature, then finely chop it. Set it aside.

4. To make the mousse, place 2⅓ cups chopped chocolate in a medium-size bowl that's set over a pot of steaming (but not boiling) water. While heating it, stir it every now and then until all the chocolate is melted, then remove the chocolate from the heat and set it aside. (Make sure no water gets into the chocolate, as this will cause the chocolate to stiffen.)

5. Whip the cream until it's thick and firm peaks form, then set it aside.

6. Whisk the eggs and triple sec in a large bowl, then set this mixture over the pot of steaming water, beating it until the mixture has tripled in volume; this could take 8–10 minutes. The eggs will be very light and creamy in appearance. Don't walk away or leave the eggs sitting over the steaming water, as this

will leave you with scrambled eggs, and you will need to start the egg process all over again.

7. Once the eggs have cooked and tripled in volume, add the melted chocolate and mix well. Fold in the cream, one-third at a time, until it's well incorporated.

8. If you'll be serving this in individual molds, pipe or scoop the mousse into the desired vessel, tapping the bowl down to create a flat surface. Place it into the refrigerator for an hour to set.

9. Melt the remaining ½ cup chopped dark chocolate in a clean dry bowl over steaming water, stirring it every now and then until it is smooth. Set aside to cool a bit, then pour a thin layer of melted dark chocolate over the chilled mousse. Return it to the fridge before serving.

10. To serve the mousse, top each portion with a little whipped cream, a scattering of the walnut praline, and a pinch of sea salt flakes. If there's praline left over, it will keep well for three months in an airtight container in the freezer.

STRAWBERRIES, BITTERSWEET CHOCOLATE, AND MAPLE-SMOKED BACON

I seem to be turning more American by the day. *Who would have thought I would be promoting bacon and chocolate together?!* It's so bad . . . and yet it's *so* good! I blame Michael Symon for sparking my love of bacon in desserts; it's impossible to pass up a serving of his maple bacon ice cream at Lola Bistro in Cleveland, Ohio! If bacon is not your thing and you want to take the vegetarian route, replace the bacon with a little sprinkling of sea salt flakes. This is the sort of dessert you can put together at the last minute.

SERVES 4

½ cup finely chopped bacon (I like a thick-cut, maple-smoked bacon)
½ cup cream
1 cup dark chocolate pieces
2 small baskets hulled, cleaned strawberries

1. In a medium-size frying pan over a medium to low heat, cook the sliced bacon, mixing it every now and then as the fat is released and the bacon starts to cook and dry out; this process will take 8–10 minutes. (Do take your time with this process, because going low and slow on the temperature will leave you with a much nicer product.) Once the bacon is cooked and there is a definite separation of fat from the bacon, remove it from the heat and set it to drain over a sieve or strainer. Lay the bacon out on paper towels to absorb a little more fat.

2. Meanwhile, place the cream in a small saucepan over medium heat and bring it to a simmer. Remove it from the heat and add the chocolate; using a whisk, beat the chocolate and cream until it's a homogeneous and thick consistency. Add the bacon and mix.

3. Serve the chocolate in little pots alongside a serving of strawberries.

CHOCOLATE PAVLOVA
WITH FRESH CREAM
AND POMEGRANATE

Both Australia and New Zealand claim the pavlova as a national dish, and stories abound as to the history of its creation. Both countries do agree, however, that the dish was named after the famous Russian ballerina Anna Pavlova. Essentially, this dessert is a baked meringue that's topped with fresh cream and fruit. I have kept this iconic dessert simple with the addition of chocolate and pomegranate. When it comes to decoration, however, look to seasonal fruit such as kiwifruit, berries, and passion fruit.

MAKES 12 SMALL PORTIONS

4 egg whites
¼ teaspoon cream of tartar
Pinch of salt
½ teaspoon white vinegar
1 cup granulated sugar
1 teaspoon cornstarch
1 tablespoon confectioners' sugar
3 drops vanilla extract
2 heaping tablespoons dark cocoa powder
1 cup freshly whipped cream
Fresh pomegranate seeds for garnish

1. Preheat the oven to 250°F (120°C). Line a baking sheet with aluminum foil or parchment paper.

2. Using an electric mixer or hand mixer on medium speed, beat the egg whites with cream of tartar and salt until they become thick and foamy.

3. Increase the speed to high, add the vinegar, and gradually add the granulated sugar in five separate batches, beating well between each addition. Continue beating until stiff peaks have formed and the sugar has dissolved. Sift in the cornstarch and confectioners' sugar, then thoroughly fold in the vanilla.

4. Remove a cup's worth of the meringue and put it in a clean bowl. Sift the cocoa powder over the meringue, mix it in thoroughly, and then carefully fold this mixture back into the white meringue. The goal is to keep some of the marbled effect in the meringue.

5. Using a tablespoon, scoop up a large spoonful of the meringue, and use a clean finger on your other hand to push the meringue onto a tray lined with foil or parchment paper. Repeat, leaving a 2-inch gap between all the meringues.

6. Place the meringues into the oven and bake them for 1 hour. Reduce the temperature to 160°F (70°C) and cook them for another 30–60 minutes or until they're dry to the touch. Turn off the oven, leaving the meringues in the oven for at least another hour or even overnight. To store the meringues, place them into an airtight container; they will stay perfectly fresh for 2–3 days.

7. To serve, place the meringues on a plate and top them with fresh whipped cream and a scattering of fresh pomegranate seeds.

CONCLUSION

Cooking is something that we do to feed nostalgia and emotions and, more important, to nourish and feed our souls as well as our bodies. Amid these goals, the ingredients we choose dictate the way we feel, function, and interact. Sometimes it can seem like a tall order to get it right. Since adopting a gluten-free lifestyle, I have unshackled myself from the chains of tiredness, exhaustion, and inflammation, including the ever-present puffy face and the belly bulge.

What I have enjoyed most is getting back to my roots of growing up on a farm, keeping mealtimes simple, eating as cleanly and as greenly as possible. My years spent learning and understanding "the French kitchen" have given me the tools to not only cook and eat well but also to connect with food and people. With this book, I am making it my goal to feed you well and to impart the importance of getting back to the table, to sharing delicious and nutritious meals with friends and family.

In all my years as a cook, I have learned that the key to a healthy lifestyle is to eat a wide variety of colors from Mother Nature's garden (and a little bit of dirt won't hurt). I have also come to appreciate just how necessary exercise, good-quality rest, loads of water, and healthy breathing patterns are for living an optimal lifestyle and feeling my best. (You'll find one of my own shorter workouts in the appendix; it's a great investment in your health with a minimal time commitment.)

I hope *Good Food—Fast!* is a cookbook that will get a genuine workout in your kitchen, that the pages get grubby with overuse, and that you find at least one recipe that becomes your personal go-to dish. I'm also hoping that by taking the time to prepare some of the more labor-intensive dishes that yield many servings, you'll have delicious leftovers that can gain a new life in another dish the following day; this will save you time and effort in the long run and still provide you with very good food. I'm looking forward to taking this health-promoting, taste-bud-satisfying journey together. If you have any questions, send them my way at Info@chefjasonroberts.com. *Cheers!*

APPENDIX: MY EXERCISE PLAN

I used to think that fitness was derived from a fifty-fifty attitude: 50 percent healthy food, 50 percent exercise. In my mind, this approach allowed for days of eating junk food and days where I didn't need to exercise. It sounds reasonable in theory, right? Boy, was I wrong!

As I have crept up in age, I have really started to believe that you need to be consistent with your efforts to achieve the best results from your body, both mentally and physically. Now I feel that the right approach is more like 100 percent food and 100 percent exercise, and that I need to be quite specific with both choices. Given the amount of training I do with running, cycling, and swimming, I have to be conscious of the foods I choose, not only for energy and body maintenance but also for recovery. Too much of certain foods (such as sugar and processed starches) creates inflammation and therefore slows down the speed of recovery after an intense exercise session. I don't want to delve too far into the science of all this, but I do want to acknowledge the reality that food and exercise go hand in hand in a healthy lifestyle.

While you may lead a chaotic lifestyle, or just have days where you feel like you can't be bothered to exercise, I want to encourage you to think about dedicating 15 minutes to moving well and making those minutes count. Every training session I have done with my trainer Greg (aka the Polish butcher) has had a purpose—the function of our muscles is essentially that purpose. There are many different definitions of functional fitness training, but for me it means to fully control my body weight in all planes of movement. Taking this approach has helped me develop strength, speed, and agility, which are used to coordinate all my body movements and improve my ability to move my body in different positions (extended, flexed, and so on) as well as through changes in planes of motion (forward and backward, side to side, rotationally).

To be honest, I didn't realize how important core strength was until my lower back started to give me grief when I would run or cycle. Now I dedicate a lot of time and effort to core training; even when I'm just walking, I will mentally activate my core muscles, therefore changing my posture. I really want to encourage you to strengthen and engage your core and understand its functionality. This will help you while you're cooking in the kitchen, eating in the dining room, and moving through everyday life.

Just like eating, exercise is something that needs to be done in moderation. The following 15-minute workout is dedicated to you and your well-being. These basic exercises have really played a key part in

MEET GREG, AKA THE POLISH BUTCHER.

my fitness level. They are simple enough that you can do them pretty much anywhere. Considering the amount of travel I do, and the inconsistencies I have with my regular exercise sessions, these 15 minutes have helped me stay on track and focused! The only equipment I carry with me are a jump rope and resistance bands.

Here is my "Full Body in 15 Workout"—thanks to my good friend, trainer, cycling partner, confidant (and sometimes torturer!) Greg Wasilczyk. He certainly knows how to get the most out of 15 minutes. My workout motto is *Just be better than when you started!* This workout will help you get there. Enjoy!

- **1 minute jumping rope:** This increases your heart rate and warms up your muscles.

- **10 full lunges (5 on each side):** This will stretch and strengthen your quadriceps and hip flexors. As you step forward into a lunge, if you raise your arms straight out above your head, you will feel a stretch throughout your lower back as well.

- **15 push-ups:** This strengthens your upper body (including your chest and upper back muscles, as well as your biceps and triceps) and builds core strength (since your abs are engaged). If doing 15 full push-ups is too hard for you, drop to your knees and do them from there, but definitely start on your toes.

- **6 lunges (3 on each side):** This time hold your arms out straight, with your hands together, then rotate at the hip to your left as far as you can comfortably stretch and then to your right. This movement allows you to feel a stretch throughout your lower back, as well as in the quadriceps and hip flexors.

- **15 chair dips:** This is a great workout for your triceps as well as your shoulders. Start by sitting on the edge of a chair with your feet together. Place your hands on the edge of the seat on either side of your thighs, scoot your bottom forward off the seat, and keep your feet planted on the ground and your back straight. Bend your elbows at a 90-degree angle and lower yourself slowly toward the floor then push yourself back up.

- **15 full squats while holding a resistance band:** The idea is to row at the same time, working your shoulders, arms, legs, and buttocks while engaging your core muscles! In a standing position, with your feet shoulder-width apart and pointing straight ahead, hold onto a resistance band that is secured (from the middle so you can pull both handles) to something stable, such as a fixed pole or a closet doorjamb at chest height; you want to make sure there is enough tension on the band so that when you row, you feel the pull! In a standing position, while facing the band, grasp the handles in front of you and lift your elbows to shoulder level; pull the band's handles back behind you, squeezing the shoulder blades together at the same time. Then lower yourself into a full squat (getting as close to a 90-degree bend in your knees as possible); at the bottom, rest for a second on your haunches, then return to standing position. Do a total of 15 repetitions.

- **10 stretch and twist moves:** This one's for your core! Plant your feet about shoulder-width apart, stand so that one side of your body is to the side of a resistance band (it should be attached to a stable structure at chest height—see above), and grasp the band with both hands. Rotate your body in the opposite direction, pulling the band across the chest while engaging your core muscles, then return to center. Do 10 on this side; then shift your body and do 10 on the other side.

- **30-second plank:** This is a simple but powerful move for your core. Hold a plank position (with your weight balanced on your forearms and on your toes) while counting slowly to 30. (I personally count sheep jumping a fence.) Pull your belly button to your spine and don't forget to breathe!

- **15 bridges:** These are for your core, lower back, and glutes. Lie on your back, with your knees bent at a 90-degree angle, your feet planted firmly on the ground and your hands,

palms down, by your thighs on the floor. Slowly raise your hips toward the ceiling, being conscious of holding your core tight and thinking about drawing your belly button toward your spine. Pause at the top of the bridge then return to the starting position. Do this 15 times.

- **20 alternating arm and leg movements:** Lie on your belly with your arms extended on the floor above your head and your legs extended straight down. While keeping your core engaged, lift your left arm and your right leg a few inches off the ground; hold this raised position for 2 seconds, then lower. Switch sides. Do a total of 10 on each side.

Rest for 1 minute, then do it all again! When you're ready to increase the intensity of this workout, I recommend adding these:

- **10 burpees (after the minute you spend jumping rope):** Not only will this give you a great cardiovascular workout but this move engages pretty much every muscle in your body. In a standing position, with your feet shoulder-width apart, lower yourself into a squatting position and place both hands on the ground in front of you. In a single move, kick both feet back so that you are suddenly in a push-up position (keep your hands firmly on the ground to support your body); lower your chest toward the ground to do

a full push-up, then kick your feet in toward your hands so you're back in the original squatting position. Stand straight up, and jump up into the air while clapping your hands above your head; return to standing. Repeat.

- **10 squat jumps (after the 15 squat rows):** This is another cardio boost and a challenge for your lower body. To do these, start in a standing position and bend your knees slightly. Lower yourself into a squat, while keeping your hips drawn back, your back straight, and your head facing forward. Think of your legs as springs, and jump up toward the ceiling as high as you can, with your hands extended upward as your feet leave the ground. Land in the same position as you started, but on the balls of your feet to cushion your landing. Swing your arms behind you (to propel yourself) and repeat immediately.

ACKNOWLEDGMENTS

Stacey Colino, my copilot: Your ability to translate my riddles and a million and one thoughts that would just fall out of my mouth over long phone conversations and cold coffee has been amazing! Your advice and fine-tuning have made this book a success. You're a dream to work with—I'm looking forward to our next project. Let's kick a few more out of the park!

Sami J., my #everever friend: Thank you for your professionalism and your ability to keep me on track, when all I wanted to do was chase you around the table. Your vision for this book and your ability to capture my love for food and my love for people and peace was a true joy to watch unfold. You're a dream to work with, a dream to create with. Here's to many more ideas, creations, and coconut waters. xo

Ty Ty: A big thank you, sweetheart, to you for allowing your mum to travel so far to be here in America to make this cookbook come to life! Your love, laughs, and sweet dance moves are always welcome in the kitchen. xo

Ahhhh, Hunter, "my boy": I didn't realize how much you would effect change in my world as you have gotten older. The way I cook and associate with life and people is big—thanks to you! It's hard living so far away from you, but I'm thankful for our weekly chats on Face Time and our time together over school holidays! I'm so proud of you; I love the young man you are growing into. Just be you; you will always be the star in my world!

Lauren Lapenna, stylish stylist and prop shopper extraordinaire: I have loved our time working together. Getting to know you and seeing you create such poetry in an image is an asset to the team! Millions of text messages and e-mails, lots of focus, lots of laughs—let's do it all again!

Gwen Benson, our city forager: I loved your ability to find things that should not have been found. No challenge was too big, no distance too far. . . . Thank you for your assistance and calmness. Ohhhh, and all the coffee to help us through this crazy shoot schedule.

Katherine Lough: I will never understand how you managed to get so much in my fridge. Thank you for your time and love for this project.

My family: Big thanks to you for dealing with me from the other side of the world; I think about you guys every day! You inspire me constantly; the distance drives me to be the best I can be in all areas of my life! Thanks, guys. I'm looking forward to sitting with you all and sharing a bowl of Nana's Rissolia.

Eric and Molly German, my Cleveland parents: I can't thank you guys enough for your continual love and support of everything that I have going on. I really look up to you; your words of love, encouragement, and advice have helped me so much over the years. Friends forever.

Greg Wasilczyk (aka the Polish butcher, aka my trainer and cycling coach, aka my friend and now my neighbor): I really have enjoyed getting to know you and your family over the last couple of years, not just because of your time and commitment to train and educate me but because of the hours you put into encouraging me! You make every day worth coming to the gym. No one else asks me, "How is the world's most beautiful athlete?" and no one else cooks kielbasa like you do! Your methods for rehydrating are second to none! The Full Body in 15 Workout still kicks my butt. I love this plan. Thank you for allowing me to share this with the world!

To my good friend and mentor Damien Pignolet: I want to thank you for your continuous support and love for the crazy craft I seem to live and call my life. I do miss our late afternoon meetings, menu planning, taste testing, and just good old chats about anything and everything! You have been a constant support and a wealth of knowledge in my culinary world. I want to acknowledge you, not just as a friend but as the amazing mentor you continue to be. Thank you for this world of food, DP!

Jacques and Claudine Pépin: I appreciate you allowing me to use your baked apple recipe in this book. Our time in Cleveland, Ohio, on stage at the Fab Food Show may have been short, but it was definitely magic. To me, your mentorship and acknowledgment is so important. I do hope we get the chance to bump shoulders again.

Darren Bettencourt, my brother from another mother: You took me under your wing. I really value our friendship and times chatting. It really was you who got this big ole ball rolling. Thank you.

The team at IMG, Sharon Chang, Ryan Dow, and Melissa Baron: Just a quick thank-you to you for continuing to open doorways for team ChefJasonRoberts. You guys have been a dream to work with, and you help me keep on brand!

Tom Howing, my big brother and good friend from Grand Rapids, Michigan: Your friendship and continued support does not go unnoticed! I'm still working on those two Emmy tickets!

J. L. Stermer and Sammy Bina and the team at N. S. Beinstock, Inc.: Thank you for building relationships and really bringing this book to life. I have loved how organically this book has come together! Your vision and guidance is truly appreciated! What's next???

Globe Pequot (Lyon Press): Without you there is no book! Thank you for understanding my love for and need to do this project and your ability to really pull a rabbit out of the hat at the last minute. I remember the day I walked into the office to meet the team in Connecticut: It was only a few minutes before we were chatting like old friends. This book was not only a quick but also a creative, organic process! You are incredibly fun and professional to work with. Thank you.

Louis Luzzo, my biggest pain in the butt: But in saying that, you are also a forever, loyal friend who will tell me when I need to pull my head in. I really value our friendship. . . . Now tweet the heck out of this book, will ya!

Team No Kid Hungry: Thank you Deb and Billy Shore for allowing me to jump onboard with No Kid Hungry. Thank you for believing in me and allowing this bucket-list project—#ChefsCycle4NKH—to even take place. (I can't believe I'm about to ride across America! I wonder if my legs will be sore after two months on a bike?) This world needs more of you guys, people who acknowledge that children are our biggest commodity and should not go hungry! This will not just be a venture across the country to raise money and awareness; this is about sharing the strength to make sure no kid goes hungry anywhere. Thank you for opening my eyes to this essential issue and this amazing charity!

My Amway family: Guys, I just wanted to thank you for your continual support, love, and encouragement! I have loved the travel and the friendships that have been forged over the years because of the opportunities you continue to lay in front of me! As for Bodykey, that was the game changer in my life: It was this product, this opportunity, that made me strive to know more, learn more, and teach more. May it live forever and continue to change people's lives.

Thank you to Pasquale and the team at PID Floors for opening their doors and floors to me and allowing me to use some of the many surfaces we shot this book on. Who would have thought that a chance meeting at the 2014 *Architectural Digest* show in NYC would have led to new friendships?! Appreciate you guys—cheers!

Team Orgreenic: A quick thanks to Marvin Levy and A. J. Khabani, my Burgan County Cycling team! I love that we have had the ability to mix business with pleasure! Nonstick ceramic pans and cycling all the way, boys.

And lastly, team accounting at Levy and Rowe: Joel Levy, Carroll Myers, and Jennifer Meynard, thank you for the countless e-mails, bills, invoices, questions, and time you've spent with me. Without you, team ChefJasonRoberts just doesn't function. Thank you for the years of effort you have put into keeping this puppy floating.

INDEX

ABOUT THE AUTHORS

New Zealand–born, New York City–based **Jason Roberts** is an internationally known celebrity chef, cookbook author, and former cast member of the hit daytime talk show *The Chew* on ABC. Roberts grew up in a family of food professionals and discovered a passion for food at an early age. He spent seven years as an executive chef in Australia, and in 2005 hosted the food talk show, *Jason Roberts' Taste* on the PAX Television Network. Roberts authored two critically acclaimed cookbooks, *Elements* and *Graze: Lots of Little Meals Fast.* Roberts's outgoing personality and energetic stage presence is a hit on the international culinary event circuit as well. His popularity has led to numerous television appearances and lucrative endorsement deals. Roberts is the brand ambassador for the world's best-selling line of cookware, Orgreenic, and in 2013 he was hired as the international spokesperson for BodyKey by Nutrilite, an award-winning healthy living and wellness program from Amway. Roberts is a big supporter of nonprofit organizations and was chosen as a celebrity advocate for No Kid Hungry, a campaign developed by the powerful nonprofit Share Our Strength. He lives in Jersey City, New Jersey.

Stacey Colino is a writer, specializing in health, weight management, and psychological issues. Her work has appeared in the *Washington Post*'s Health section and in dozens of national magazines, including *Newsweek, Real Simple, Health, MORE, Women's Health, Prevention, Woman's Day, Redbook, Self, Elle, Harper's Bazaar, Marie Claire, Glamour, Shape, Parents,* and *Ladies' Home Journal.* She has been a contributing editor to *Child, Remedy, Weight Watchers* magazine, and *American Health for Women.* She is the coauthor with David L. Katz, MD, of *Disease-Proof*; the coauthor of *Taking Back the Month*; and the coauthor with Jennifer Cohen of *Strong Is the New Skinny.* She has received dozens of awards for her writing and lives with her family in Chevy Chase, Maryland.